In marketing today, delusional thinking
isn't just acceptable, it's mandatory.

MARKETERS ARE FROM
MARS
CONSUMERS ARE FROM
NEW JERSEY

BOB HOFFMAN

Marketers Are From Mars, Consumers Are From New Jersey by Bob Hoffman

Cover Design: Bonnie Miguel
Interior Design: Bonnie Miguel
Publisher: Type A Group, LLC
For information contact bob@typeagroup.com

ISBN 978-1508977117

Also by
BOB HOFFMAN

The Ad Contrarian

101 Contrarian Ideas About Advertising

Quantum Advertising

Praise For Bob Hoffman's Writing And Speaking

"Caustic yet truthful"
The Wall Street Journal

"It's nice to find a real thinker in the ad business these days"
Jack Trout, Forbes.com

"Bob is the little child who points out that the emperor is wearing no clothes, while too many of his advertising colleagues go along with the hype because it pays their salaries. This man has a great sense of humour, plenty of relevant agency experience, courage. And his position is ethical, he cares about advertising/marketing and the consumer - the same can't be said for so many consultants peddling hype and fads to unwitting marketers....I'm jealous. I wish I'd been brave enough to be this rude."
Prof. Byron Sharp, Author "How Brands Grow"

"...fresh, surprising, in-your-face insights into how just about everything we take as gospel in advertising is wrong. What Bob Hoffman is saying is that...we're going to have to come up with a whole new language and belief system for what advertising is supposed to do, based not on clichés, but on how things really are."
Andrew Jaffe, Executive Director, Clio Awards

"I began discussing these (ideas) with agencies and staff the day after finishing the book"
Neil Golden, CMO, McDonald's

"...(Bob's) presentation on our industry was the best I've ever seen. It was smart, well written, and it was at times, hysterically funny."
Joe Erwin, President, Erwin Penland.

"...the most entertaining talk given during Advertising Week Europe (or any conference for that matter.")
AdRants

"Let me once again say - BRAVO!... a highlight of the week."
Erica Farber, President & CEO, Radio Advertising Bureau

"... the best presentation I've ever had the pleasure of witnessing, truly."
Cam Green, CEO, GreenRubino

"Bob is one of the smartest guys in the business. His thoughts are not obscured by fads, what's au courant, or quotidian bs. He is a straight-shooter. Honest, to the point and fact-based. Qualities sorely missing in the world today."
George Tannenbaum, author, Ad Aged

"This book is an insightful, hilarious look at what's wrong with advertising agencies, with marketing in general, and maybe even the world overall. But it isn't just for people who work in ad agencies. It's for anybody who ever saw an ad that sucked and wondered how it got that way. It's for anybody who works in any kind of job involving generation of new ideas. And yes, it's for anybody who enjoys "Mad Men." Bob Hoffman is smarter than Don Draper. He's funnier than Don Draper. And he's better looking than... Okay, like I said, Bob Hoffman is definitely smarter and funnier than Don Draper."
Joe Norris, CEO Emeritus, SHS

"Whether you like it or not, you now have disciples around the country who will be preaching your gospel."
Bill Lavidge, CEO, The Lavidge Company

Dedication

This book is dedicated to all the funny, cynical, immature bastards I worked with in the agency business.

It is not dedicated to all the venal, duplicitous, scheming bastards I also worked with.

Author's Notes

Most of the material in this book first appeared elsewhere.

The bulk comes from my blog, *The Ad Contrarian*. Some is taken from articles I've written for publications or talks I've given. And some of it is just stuff I found lying around at Taco Bell.

Although some of the data referred to have changed since the pieces were written, I've left most intact. Some data I have updated for clarity. I've edited some pieces to remove repetitive points, and I've edited other pieces to remove things that, in retrospect, make me seem like a real fucking idiot.

In creating a book that is essentially a compilation, one faces a problem. When writing essays each piece must stand on its own. So, for example, if I say in an essay that "interactivity with advertising is a delusion," I have to back it up with a fact — like less than 1 person in a thousand clicks on a banner ad. In a compilation, the repetition of these "proof points" can become tedious. I have tried to minimize them, but I recognize that, of necessity, some points are made more than once. Sorry.

I want to thank Bonnie Miguel for the design and formatting of the book, as well as her infinite patience, and Sharon Krinsky for many ideas that appear here, including the idea that lead to the title.

I also want to thank Mia for not throwing me out a window.

Contents

Foreword

If you ever have trouble falling asleep, I suggest you try writing a book. The minute the document appears on your computer screen the eyelids get heavy and the breathing slows. This is my third book and I've never been so well rested.

Like my other books, this one is mostly a compilation of stuff I wrote for other reasons. In contemporary terms this is known as re-purposing. In earlier times it was known as plagiarizing yourself. I'll let you decide which is more accurate.

My last book, *101 Contrarian Ideas About Advertising*, reached number one on the Amazon advertising paperback hit parade and stayed there for a good while. At the rates Amazon pays, my heirs should be entitled to over 120 dollars.

Since my last book I have retired from the advertising agency business and become a part-time consultant, part-time speaker, part-time writer, and part-time bum. I find I am reasonably good at the consulting, speaking, and writing, and alarmingly capable as a bum.

Fortunately, the advertising and marketing businesses haven't gotten any less silly and there is still a great deal of material for a cynical old bastard to work with.

In fact, the marketing industry is currently in the midst of a mass delusion of epic proportions. This includes the gross exaggeration of the role of brands; the mangling of the role of ad agencies; the mistaking of gimmicks for trends; the abandonment of the most powerful consumer group the world has ever seen; the wishful thinking of social media marketing; and the fraud and corruption of digital advertising. It's quite an appetizing menu.

Well, my job is to try to stick a fork in all this nonsense.

If this book goes a small way toward accomplishing that, I'll be happy and you'll be entertained. Let's go.

Chapter One:

They've landed

MARKETERS ARE FROM MARS,
CONSUMERS ARE FROM NEW JERSEY

Marketers and consumers (and by consumers I mean, ya know, people) are from different worlds.

Consumers are basically simple creatures with straightforward needs and easily observed behaviors.

Marketers are complicated critters with strange customs and mysterious beliefs.

Marketers are taught not to think simply. In fact, the whole practice of marketing is based on the conviction that there are forces at work in the minds of consumers that only trained specialists (ya know, us) are qualified to interpret.

Thinking simply has been beaten out of marketers.

You can't be taken seriously in any marketing or advertising organization if you suggest that the bulk of consumer behavior is perfectly obvious. You can't advance your career by speaking plainly and asserting the indisputable — that the reason people buy most products is because they are cheaper, tastier, prettier, work better or are simply more readily available.

That kind of thinking just won't cut it in today's world of professional confusion.

Today you need to be at least a sidewalk sociologist and, even better, a pseudo-psychiatrist to be taken seriously as a marketing professional.

In fact, you need to think and speak in ways that no consumer in the history of civilization has ever thought or spoken. How marketers think and how consumers think couldn't be more different.

How marketers think:

How can I engage consumers with my brand?

How do I connect the personality of my brand with my target audience?

How can I co-create with my target and develop a conversation?

How consumers think:

Is there parking?

Will this fucking thing work?

How badly are they going to screw me on the price?

Will there be anyone there who knows what the fuck he's talking about?

Consumers want clarity and simplicity. Marketers want to complicate the shit out of everything.

BOZOS IN THE BOARDROOM

In a more discerning age, entertainers were called *fools*. Today, entertainers have become oracles.

Marketers have always been willing to pay entertainers for the reflected glory of their fame. Now they're willing to invite these people into the board room.

Celebrities like Beyonce, Taylor Swift, Justin Timberlake, Lady Gaga, Robert Downey, Jr. and Alicia Keys are being paid by marketers to be part of the corporate structure. Or at least, to pretend to be.

According to *Ad Age*, *"..brands aren't just featuring celebs in marketing campaigns — they're giving stars a place in the marketing suite...with lofty titles like chief creative officer (and)...chief innovator..."*

The idea that entertainers belong in the corporate structure is exceptionally silly.

Let's start with actors. Actors are good at pretending. Their talent is making believe. They can pretend they are Jesus, or cowboys, or Iron Man, or Abraham Lincoln. But here's the thing. They are not Jesus, or cowboys, or Iron Man, or Abraham Lincoln. They are mostly just ninnies who are good at pretending.

Then there are singers. The ability to sing is a lovely and pleasant talent. However, it is a talent that has no correlation to any other attribute. The ability to sing makes you no more virtuous, intelligent, or insightful than your average dry cleaner. It would not surprise us to learn that Joseph Goebbels had a lovely baritone.

Qualities totally unrelated to acting and singing have been attributed to these people. As our pandering media pay more and more attention to celebrities' idiotic shenanigans, they continue to gain status in the shallow, injudicious culture of our industry.

Enter Will.i.am. About 18 months ago Will.i.am began blazing the trail for celebrity marketing poseurs. If you are not a fan of hip-hop and pop culture, Will.i.am is a very successful music entrepreneur. He fronted the Black Eyed Peas, produced for huge stars, won Grammies and has loads of platinum.

He is also known for one of the worst half-time shows in Super Bowl history (nothing will ever be worse than The Who.) At the time, he was also responsible for creating some Super Bowl spots for Salesforce.com which were, remarkably, even worse than his half-time show.

Will followed his Super Bowl megaflops with a blog piece about marketing in Ad Age called *"What Does Communiting Mean?"*

It was so stupefyingly dumb that I don't even know how to begin to describe it. It was written in a kind of post-literate, faux-poetic style that might impress the dimmest 12-year-old.

The whole piece had the tone of those YouTube videos from a couple of years ago about social media (the ones that breathlessly explained how there are more people on Facebook than there are in the entire universe.) Then we were treated to a painful stream of Will's infantile philosophizing...

"...today is all about accessing the physical representation of collective consciousness"

Really? But can I still watch hockey?

"...you need to create conversations with your customers...so I say, MAKE CONVERSATIONS NOT ADS..."

Wow, an amazing thought.

But the real piece de resistance is a word he made up — "communiting." It's the kind of cringe-inducing neologism an 8th-grader would invent.

"...COMMUNITING is about COMMUNICATION between people and companies that enables or sustains a COMMUNITY..."

You can tell COMMUNITING is important because of the use of ALL CAPS.

In addition to being a corporate marketing advisor to Salesforce, Will.i.am also holds the title of Director of Creative Innovation at Intel. It's starting to feel like Silicon Valley is getting mighty thick with star-fuckers.

Recently, the Clio awards announced that Will.i.am has been awarded an "honorary award" this year for his "inspired creative work." At a recent marketing conclave, this inspiring genius had this inspiring thing to say:

"We need to stop looking at people as consumers and start looking at what they are, which is people."

Are there Clios for tautology?

The marketing industry, totally absorbed with data and metrics and completely bereft of ideas, has a new beard to hide behind — entertainers.

We've got to get these fools back into their silly hats and pointy shoes before they start doing real damage.

Ill.i.am.

THE COCOON OF IGNORANCE AT CANNES

For sheer stupidity, it's hard to beat Keats' famous assertion that...

"Beauty is truth, truth beauty..."

But Yahoo ceo Marissa Mayer took a nice swing at it at the Cannes egofest this week by asserting that... *"Art is advertising and advertising is art."*

Apparently Ms. Mayer hasn't visited her website recently. As I write this, here's the "art" that is on display in the upper right quadrant of my Yahoo home page:

Man, this is some artistic shit.

Now, it's pretty clear what Marissa is up to here. She's obviously out to kiss the asses of the overfed peacocks who, this time every year, turn Cannes into a grotesque carnival of wastefulness and self-congratulation. There's nothing that makes a self-worshipping ad poser glow and buzz like being told he's an artist.

Marissa then demonstrated a degree of cluelessness about advertising unmatched, even by a tech ceo... *"Digital advertising needs to aspire to be as good as art and then some."*

Yo, M — I got some news for you. In the septic tank that is the ad industry, digital advertising is the stuff flopping around at the bottom.

Aspire to be art? This stuff barely aspires to be dirt.

Advertising has always been 90% lousy, but online advertising has set a new standard for awfulness.

The fact that a ceo of one of the world's largest media companies believes digital advertising needs to "be as good as art and then some" tells you something about the cocoon of fantasy and delusion these people live in.

M— just a word of advice from an old hand at this game. Be careful what you say in public. People might think you're serious.

EVERYTHING NOT PREVIOUSLY DEAD IS NOW DEAD

Guess what? Now marketing is dead, too!

First television was dead. Then advertising was dead.

Now marketing is dead.

This time it must be true because it comes from some genius who teaches at Stanford and writes for the Harvard Business Review. It seems like the gaudier the credentials, the dopier the patter (stolen directly from one of my all-time favorite lines: Sam Spade, in The Maltese Falcon says, "The cheaper the crook, the gaudier the patter.")

You can read about the terrible death of marketing (such a pity, it was so young) on a website called *Yes and Know* (groan.) The name of the piece in question is *What Replaces Marketing?* Apparently, the answer is "shared purpose" (double-extra-groan.)

You see, we ad hacks are no longer responsible for selling stuff, instead we are social workers whose job is to "engage in a community" and "co-create with people."

After feeding us this baloney sandwich, the writer goes off into hyperspace about Apple retail stores, completely misunderstanding Apple's business strategy. If ever there was a secretive, paranoid, walled culture that absolutely, positively refused to "engage in a community" or "co-create with people" it's Apple.

But you really can't appreciate the depths of the cluelessness of this meatball until you hear her advice for Best Buy on how to resurrect their rapidly decomposing carcass...

"...become social thru Pinterest... all of a sudden you become a magnet for what's hot."

All of a sudden! Wow, that was easy! Man, this marketing stuff is fun!

I know that the people who write all these insufferable "_____ is Dead" articles are imbeciles, but please, when will the Guardians Of The Internet stop publishing this crap? Who the hell is in charge here?

HYPOCRISY BY PROXY

There is a horrible medical syndrome called Munchausen By Proxy. In it, a mentally ill parent invents or induces medical symptoms in a child to gain attention for herself (in 85% of cases it's a mother.)

Earlier this week, in a post called *Munchausen by Proxy by Media* Seth Godin compared Munchausen By Proxy to what our media does to viewers. According to Seth...

> *"...the media does this to us all the time... It started a century ago with the Spanish American War. Disasters sell newspapers. And a moment-by-moment crisis gooses cable ratings, and horrible surprises are reliable clickbait. The media rarely seeks out people or incidents that encourage us to be calm, rational or optimistic...*
>
> *Even when they're not actually causing unfortunate events, they're working to get us to believe that things are on the brink of disaster."*

Seth's point is undeniably true. By turning events into "crises" the media draws attention to itself, and earns a nice little profit from the increased viewership/listenership/readership.

I would like to suggest that this is also a perfect description of what some of Seth's pals in the marketing punditocracy have done for the past 15 years.

Since about 2000, the marketing establishment has been engaged in creating phony crises based on flimsy evidence, questionable assertions, and exaggerated claims:

- the death of traditional advertising
- the death of television
- the death of the "interruption model"
- the end of mass marketing

- the enthusiasm of consumers for "interacting" with advertising
- the miracle of social media

The "thought leaders" of the marketing industry are no less guilty of playing the hysteria card to buy themselves status (and consulting gigs) than the media are.

The more they can convince us that everything is changing — and we need them to interpret the changes — the longer they stay employed. And so they have created an avalanche of exaggerated claims and dire warnings that gain them attention and a nice little profit from the increased viewership / listenership / readership.

Creating alarm is just plain good strategy — whether it's by the media or those who choose to criticize it.

THERE'S NO BULLSHIT LIKE BRAND BULLSHIT

Okay, just for the record let's state the obvious:

- Yes, having a strong brand is very valuable.
- Yes, the highest goal of advertising is to create a strong brand.

Now, let's get to the bullshit

- No, for the most part consumers are not in love with brands
- No, consumers do not want to have a conversation with your brand, or an "authentic relationship" with it, or co-create with it, or engage with it, or dance with it, or take a shower with it.

They want it to work well, taste good, be reasonably priced, and look pretty. End of story.

As I've said about a million times (and Prof. Byron Sharp has said much more articulately in his book, *How Brands Grow*) most of what we call "brand loyalty" is simply habit, convenience, mild satisfaction or easy availability.

I promise you, if Pepsi would disappear tomorrow, most Pepsi "loyalists" would switch over to Coke with very little psychological damage.

Nike devotees would throw on a pair of Adidas without having to enter rehab.

McDonald's faithfuls would cheerfully eat a Whopper without the need for counseling.

In fact, according to Havas Media, *"in Europe and the US, people would not care if 92% of brands disappeared."* And, to be perfectly honest here, I would not care if Havas Media disappeared.

Which brings us to a lovely bit of new age marketing baloney published on the *Entrepreneur* website recently called *"How to Get Customers Raving About Your Brand"*

Apparently, in the never-never-land of brand babble, the way you get customers "raving" about you is through *transparency*, or to quote the article, *"transparency is the new black."*

You see, consumers are now so enchanted by their love of brands that they are studying brands to see which ones are most transparent.

This makes it a little difficult to explain the world's most successful company — Apple — which, with the possible exception of North Korea, is the most secretive enterprise in the history of mankind.

Apparently, opaque is the new transparent.

The meatball who wrote this thing thinks Starbuck's is successful because of its transparency. On the other hand, I have a feeling it might have something to do with having a store on every corner, making the stores clean and comfortable, and serving a good cup of coffee.

In fact, I did a little survey at my local Starbuck's this morning. I went around and asked everybody why they were there. Transparency came up exactly... hang on, let me check my notes... oh, here it is — no times.

But this is the new ideological world of marketing. Marketing is no longer about meeting the practical needs of customers. It's about high-minded principles of transparency and co-creating and conversations and...

Well, I'm afraid I have a very old guy opinion. You want customers raving about your brand? Sell them a good fucking product.

BRAND, BULLSHIT, AND BEYOND

Recently, the Ad Contrarian blog has been breaking all kinds of attendance records.

In trying to analyze the reason for this sudden popularity, I've noticed something. People seem to love posts with the word "bullshit" in the title.

Being the kind of guy who likes to give the customer what she wants, from now on the title of every post will contain the word "bullshit." I think this is what CMOs call "best practices."

Speaking of bullshit, last week, I really gave it to the Global CEO of a huge ad agency concerning a video he did in which he invoked the genius of Steve Jobs for his own purposes — and got it 100% wrong.

The guy was lecturing on his theory called *"Why Your Brand Is More Important Than Your Product"* which, of course, is the constant mantra of the world's professional brand babblers. To bolster his theory he referenced Steve Jobs and proclaimed that the reason for Steve's great success was that he, too, followed this religion.

Only problem was that Mr. Global was absolutely, positively, laughably wrong. In fact, Steve was such a believer in the power of the product that according to Allison Johnson, Apple's *VP of Worldwide Marketing*, at Apple "brand" was a "dirty word" and Steve "dreaded, hated" the word "branding."

Now we get an equally powerful repudiation of the misrepresentations of this global loudmouth, this time from the man who was closest to Steve at Apple, Jony Ive.

The New Yorker has a lengthy and interesting profile of Ive called *"The Shape of Things to Come: How an industrial designer became Apple's greatest product."*

Here are some quotes from the piece juxtaposed with some of the assertions of Mr. Global.

Steve Jobs: "If I had a spiritual partner at Apple, it's Jony. Jony and I think up most of the products together and then pull the others in and say 'Hey, what do you think about this?' He gets the big picture as well as the most infinitesimal details about each product. And he understands that Apple is a product company."

Global CEO: "Product first, I think, is very retro and very 1980's."

Jony Ive: "I can't emphasize enough: I think there's something really very special about how practical we are. And you could, depending on your vantage point, describe it as old school and traditional, or you could describe it as very effective."

Global CEO: (About Jobs) He started with an idea that consumers want to be bespoke...and he back-filled into a product.

Ive: "We put the product ahead of everything else."

Don't you love it? There is so much bullshit in our business. Most of it arrives in the form of an opinion or an anecdote. Consequently, it is very hard to actually catch a bullshitter red-handed like this.

I don't know why this thrills me so much, but it does. Despite all my tantrums, I really do feel deeply about the ad business and I'm sick at heart from watching it being diminished and dismantled by financial manipulators and insufferable blowhards.

I'm also completely tired of these over-fed meatballs undermining the credibility of our industry with their trite, cunning theories and pompous pronouncements.

Thank you Allison Johnson and Jony Ive.

WHAT THE BRAND BABBLERS DON'T UNDERSTAND

Imagine for a second that you're the brand manager for BigSave super-markets.

Your job is to build the BigSave brand so that customers prefer you to SaveMore, and HugeSave.

You know how wonderful BigSave is. You want to spread the word. You want consumers to see inside your brand. You want them to know how responsive you are, and how pleasant you are to engage with, and how willing you are to work with them and help them.

Building the BigSave brand is absolutely essential to your career and central to your life. Once you leave the house in the morning, it is the most important thing you do.

Now let's talk about the average consumer. The average con-sumer couldn't give a flying shit about BigSave.

If BigSave exploded tomorrow, the average consumer wouldn't bother picking up the donuts.

The average consumer has other things on her mind. Like why she gained two pounds last week, and why her father is looking pale, and why the fucking computer keeps losing its WiFi signal, and why Timmy's teacher wants to see her, and what's that bump she noticed on her arm?

The point is this: our brands are very important to us marketers and very unimportant to most consumers. Please read that again.

Are there some brands each of us are attached to? Sure. Are there brands we buy regularly? Sure. Is our attachment to a handful of brands strong and emotional? Sure. The problem is we buy stuff in hundreds of categories and are strongly attached to only a few brands.

The idea that our attachment represents "love" or any of the other woolly nonsense perpetrated by brand hustlers is folly.

The clearest demonstration of the weakness of the cult of brands is the dismal performance of social media marketing. We were promised that social media would be the magic carpet on which our legions of brand advocates would go to spread the word about the marvelousness of our brands, and would free us from the terrible, wasteful expense of advertising. It has done nothing of the sort.

In fact, it is often the exact opposite. Social media is usually where people go to scream about the mistreatment they get at the hands of companies. And where companies go to beg forgiveness.

Having a successful brand is very important to a marketer. But the idea that it is anything like that to a consumer is folly. Brand babble is just the faulty conflation of marketers' needs and consumers' interests.

Modern marketing is operating under the delusion that consumers want to interact with brands, and have relationships with brands, and have brand experiences, and engage with them, and co-create with them.

Sorry, amigo. Not in this lifetime.

LET'S GET PHYGITAL

We are so used to massive bullshit in the advertising business that it really takes something special to shock us.

I'm happy to say, however, that our industry is up to the challenge. You want bullshit that's something special? We got it.

Last weekend I came across a truly outstanding exercise in painful marketing drivel, and I'm proud to share it with you.

It is hard to believe that an agency would actually allow this nonsense on its website. But not only is it on the website, it is the lead copy on their landing page and, apparently, the underpinning of their philosophy.

Buckle up:

> *"Co-creating with brands and people in the Phygital world. Modern consumers are "connected protagonists." They are the heroes of their own stories and, thanks to technology, they now have access to an audience of unprecedented size. This presents brands with powerful new opportunities for growth, if brands give consumers the currency to create and share better stories. That currency is content - be it entertainment, connection, experience or information - as long as it is created with the understanding that we live in a Phygital world, where the physical and digital parts of our lives are one and the same. We believe that only through co-creating currency with brands and people - instead of for people - can you guarantee authentic engagements that consumers value and want to share. (The agency) provides to marketers - in thought and action - the ideas that engage the connected protagonist to build value for brands and people."*

Wow. Let's forget all the usual hogwash — the co-creating, and the engaging, and the sharing, and the currency (note to author — you seem to have forgotten "ecosystem." Points off.) Let's get to the fun stuff.

The "connected protagonist." He sounds like an amiable guy with an unsevered umbilicus.

And how are you gonna beat Phygital? I mean, c'mon. It's stupiculous! It's ludiposterous! If they gave awards for just plain dumbness, Phygital would get double platinum.

Which gets me thinking. They give awards for everything else in the ad business. Why not for the only thing we really excel at — bullshit.

DELIGHTING IN DIGITAL DUMBNESS

You simply cannot make this shit up.

Just when you think the world of online advertising can't get any more absurd, the banner boys prove you wrong again.

Let's start at the beginning.

Recently, we wrote about an article in The Wall Street Journal that reported on a study by comScore which found that 54% of display ads paid for by advertisers were never seen by a live human being.

About a month ago, a digital media company created an info-graphic about this finding. Not satisfied to leave bad enough alone, they decided that it required some commentary.

Here's what these people deduced:

> *"...higher rates of viewability drive increased action through the effect of accumulated ad-views."*

For those of you who speak English, what this bullshit means is that ads you can see are more likely to be effective than ads you cannot see. How's that for a stunning insight?

Gosh, what's next? Cars with motors go faster than cars without motors? People with teeth chew better than people without teeth?

> *"With a move to marketers only paying for adverts that are seen, this infographic highlights a sea change in online advertising."*

"Marketers only paying for adverts that are seen." Huh? What kind of moron would pay for ads that are not seen? I mean, besides a CMO?

Expecting ads to be seen is apparently a radical new "approach" in the never-never-land of online advertising.

> *"Brand marketers are able to use this approach to safeguard the*

> *quality of their advertising inventory, whilst performance*
> *marketers can benefit from the increased response that is*
> *triggered by more viewable advertising."*

I don't even know what to say about this monumental stupidity. But here's the line that really got me:

> *"If an ad is in view, your audience is more likely to act upon it."*

No shit? You mean an ad works better if someone can see it? Well fuck me blind.

This astounding line of thinking exists in a world that requires a wonderful, extraordinary kind of dumbness. It takes a transcendent dumbness. It takes a dumbness that charms, and thrills, and makes you think that maybe life really is just a bowl of fucking cherries. It takes more than traditional dumbness. It takes cutting-edge, state-of-the-art, up-to-the-minute, undiluted, artisanally curated *digital* dumbness.

WHAT'S EVERYONE SO AFRAID OF?

I am sometimes approached by editors of advertising or media publications to write pieces for them. In the course of trying to convince me to contribute tendentious pieces to their publications (and not get paid!) invariably the following sentence is uttered:

"We're so tired of all the bullshit"

Often when I attend a conference and one of those gee-whiz presentations about the latest digital advertising magic is made, people will later approach me at the bar and whisper:

"What a bunch of bullshit."

(By the way, I'm at the bar because that's where they keep the pretzels.)

One recent morning I was having coffee with a person who manages media and marketing conferences and she told me that the biggest problem she has in creating interesting programs is that every presenter pretends to be a futurist guru who talks about whatever the hype-cycle-miracle-of-the-week is, and everyone else is too chicken to challenge these guys.

What I want to know is, what's everybody in advertising so afraid of ? Why won't people say what they really think? Even after 20 years of totally hysterical nonsense, are we still too timid to defend our business and stand up to these buffoons?

Why do publishers keep publishing "all the bullshit" if they're so tired of it?

Why will people only call bullshit in whispered tones in the dim confines of the hotel bar? Why won't speakers get up and speak their minds?

There is a kind of creeping, low-grade McCarthyism in the advertising world. Everyone's afraid to challenge the loudmouths. "Thought leaders" go from conference to conference being dead-wrong, and everyone is so terrified of being thought odd or old-fashioned that they refuse to speak up.

The ad industry is becoming stinkier and stinkier. And I don't know what smells worse, the bullshit or the chicken shit.

Chapter Two:

Ad Craft

THE SEARCH FOR MIRACLES

With the exceptions of pop music and fashion, there is probably no more trendy business than advertising.

Every few years we invent a trendy new miracle and everyone immediately jumps on it.

Sometimes it's a media miracle like social media.

Sometimes it's a process miracle like account planning.

Sometimes it's a technical miracle like "big data."

Whatever shape the miracle takes, one thing is for sure: it's going to change everything.

Every agency in the known universe jumps all over the new miracle and it becomes the centerpiece of their website and their new business pitch.

Every agency also becomes expert in this new miracle, and starts up a department to specialize in it. They "brand" it (i.e., give it a stupid name) and develop a pseudo-proprietary flavor of this miracle.

Although what they do is exactly the same as what every other agency does, their flavor usually contains some kind of highly-evolved methodology with circles and arrows and dotted lines and feedback loops.

In other words, it's a muy grande bullshit burrito.

Amazingly, clients believe in these miracles. The way it happens is that the agency usually trots out the example of a company that has been wildly successful implementing the miracle. The fact that this example is two or three standard deviations from normal is never discussed. All that anyone needs to know is that Zappos was a huge social media success, or "got milk" utilized account planning, or, I don't know, someone had 6 hits on their QR code, and naive clients start salivating and wanting a piece of the miracle.

The truly sad part is that there really is an advertising miracle. It's called an idea — a great creative idea. Unfortunately, this miracle is hard to come by and there are very few who can perform it.

The ad business has adopted a very dangerous and short-sighted habit: selling the wrong kind of miracles.

The only real miracle we have in our bag of tricks is the creative one. It's the only one we've ever had.

The most appropriate phrase ever written about advertising miracles was written by someone you've never heard of named Herman Hupfeld. Herman wrote,

> *"The fundamental things apply,*
> *As time goes by."*

THE POWER OF PRECISION GUESSING

We know that consumer behavior is often irrational. That's why there are large market share differences among products that are essentially the same.

We also know that consumers tend to be pragmatic and don't like to throw their money around on crap. That's why so many new products fail.

So how do we reconcile these two seeming contradictions? How can consumers be both strangely emotional yet essentially pragmatic? We can't explain it. That's what makes advertising so interesting. It's like physics. There are two equally reliable, yet contradictory ways to explain the physical behavior of matter.

General relativity describes the world one way. Quantum physics describes it another. They are completely different, and often contradictory theories. And yet each is equally capable of explaining and predicting the behavior of matter — general relativity on a large scale and quantum physics on a small scale.

We face a similar (and far less important) enigma in advertising. If you ask an advertising expert "what makes a great campaign" he/she will provide you with a list of adjectives — beautiful, persuasive, funny, entertaining, convincing... but the truth is, nobody really knows what makes a great ad campaign.

I can show you a hundred campaigns that were all of those things and failed, and you can show me a hundred that were none of them and succeeded.

The thing that drives ad people crazy, and makes advertising such a fascinating endeavor, is that there is no algorithm for great advertising. No one has been able to define the proper proportions of the emotional and the practical, the nonlinear and the utilitarian, the entertaining and the convincing.

And that leads us to the point of this piece. The present obsession with media delivery systems may help our media people locate a certain type of person more easily, but is never going to provide the spark of brilliance on how to motivate this person.

Understanding motivation still comes from the brains of talented people who somehow know what the right combination of ingredients is to motivate a certain type of person in a certain category.

They don't know how they know it, and sometimes they don't even know that they know it. But they do.

That's why there are a few people who consistently create wonderful, successful advertising and others who create consistently mediocre advertising.

It's a gift that some creative people have for precision guessing. That's all it is, but it is the amazing gift that separates real advertising talent from the rest of us.

GREAT ADVERTISING TRANSCENDS THE RULES

Yeah, yeah, yeah. We all know that advertising is 50% strategy and 50% execution. Or something like that.

But that's only true of normal advertising. The kind you and I do.

It's not true of great advertising — the kind people a thousand times better than us do.

Great advertising transcends strategy. It's great for all the wrong reasons — the reasons we never talk about in new business pitches, or mention at client meetings, or have break-out sessions about at advertising conferences. It's great because it's great. Period.

It doesn't matter if it differentiates the brand, or delivers a benefit, or has a call to action.

Good ads need strategy and benefits and differentiation. Great ads don't need any of that. They appeal to us as humans, not consumers.

It's like art or music or literature. The really good artists and musicians and writers know the rules of artistry. But the great ones say "screw the rules."

STEALING FOR SUCCESS

Back in my agency days I was a pretty good copywriter. Not great and not terrible, just pretty good.

I like to think that if I had focused more on creative work and less on agency management I could have been better. Of course, this is the kind of bullshit we all tell ourselves to excuse our mediocrity.

In my career I had a few hit campaigns (way too few). While these hits lasted a brief time, they represented the most enjoyable days I spent in advertising. It really is fun to have people talking about something you've created.

One of my hit campaigns was the result of precision stealing. I didn't steal the idea, but I borrowed a structure. By paying attention to what really good creative people do, you can learn a lot and apply it to your work.

My partner had a terrific idea for a campaign we were working on. She got the idea from a character in a movie.

But we were stuck in the "idea" stage. We couldn't figure out how to make the idea into a spot (by the way, one of the biggest problems creative people have is in not understanding the difference between an idea and a spot.)

Anyway, we were struggling. One morning I was riding down the elevator of our building when I asked myself a question: How would Hal Riney have written this spot? One minute later I had the spot done.

Riney frequently used an old film technique in which he would have a narrator weave in and out of the dialogue moving the story along. Of course, he didn't invent this structure, but he used it very effectively.

The spot we did looked nothing like anything Riney would ever write, but by borrowing the structure we made it into a good spot. In other words, we swiped something from a movie, applied a technique someone borrowed from film school, and out popped something pretty good.

Sometimes, creativity isn't about re-inventing. Sometimes it's about re-arranging.

FEAR OF SELLING

I don't want to be a salesman. I want to be an artist. I know it's not easy, but it's what I want.

If I can't be an artist, at least I want to be helpful. I want to change things. I've seen the damage that crass consumerism can do. I don't want to be a peddler. I am nobler than that.

You know what I mean, right? You agree, right?

Well, here's the thing. If you're in advertising, you're a salesman.

It doesn't matter what you think you are or what you want to be. You're a salesman. I don't like it either.

One of the problems advertising has always faced is that there are a lot of people in the business who don't want to be salespeople. They have a vested interest — a personal, self-image interest — in not thinking of themselves as salespeople. And today they have more opportunity than ever to act on this illusion.

They have convinced themselves, and many others in the marketing industry, that selling is not the purpose of advertising.

They go to conferences and write books and make presentations that tell us that the nature of consumer behavior has changed. That selling is no longer our raison d'etre.

They don't want to make ads. Ads are too graceless, too direct, and too transparently commercial. Everyone knows the motives behind ads.

They'd rather do their work behind an opaque curtain. They'd rather pretend they're not making advertising. You see, they're being helpful.

They'd rather make believe that what they're doing is a form of social intercourse. It makes them feel better. They're not here to sell you something. They just want to have a conversation and build a relationship.

They can cling to their timid, anemic illusions all they want but in the end they will be judged on how good they are at selling. Sorry, amigo, that's business.

THE UNIVERSAL CREATIVE BRIEF

Here at *The Ad Contrarian* global headquarters, we know that our friends in agencies have a big problem: How do you write a creative brief that sounds original, yet says exactly the same thing as every other brief? Not an easy task!

Consequently, we have developed a universal creative brief that can work in any situation. All you have to do is fill in the brand's name and, bingo, your brief is done and you're ready to get back to your important Facebook obligations.

UNIVERSAL CREATIVE BRIEF

Client: (_____)

Job No. XB-9901

Date: April 27, 2015

Situation:

(_____) is a beloved challenger brand. In order to maintain its relevance, we must engage the millennial target in a way that creates a cognitive and emotional connection between the brand and the target.

Key Insight:

Our millennial target is turned-off by advertising. They do not react to linear brand messages or product claims. In order to impact this consumer positively, the keys are authenticity and transparency.

Assignment:

We need to create a new communication platform for (_____). This should not be seen by the target as "advertising." In fact, we should resist the urge to create material that delivers one-way messaging. Instead, we should encourage our target to engage and co-create with us in a way that provides a framework for unified brand-target alignment.

Objectives:

1. Transition from a "functional" brand to an "emotional" brand.

2. Create a purpose-driven movement with the brand at the center.

3. Motivate an ongoing conversation between our brand and our millennial target.

4. Socialize our transparency initiative for full stakeholder buy-in.

5. Utilize data-driven insights across the brand portfolio.

Strategy:

Primary: Institute a multi-channel solution that leverages owned, earned, and bought media assets.

Secondary: Communicate the brand essence across the brand ecosystem.

Desired Outcomes:

1. Target will view us as an authentically relevant brand that is aligned with millennial social constructs and beliefs.

2. Target will understand and appreciate our transparency initiative and assign positive meaning to the brand.

Mandatories:

1. Our iconic Dancing Rabbits must appear in every piece of communication.

2. Please use the stacked logo as the client believes it has more impact than the horizontal logo.

3. "Quality <u>And</u> Value" remain at the core of our value proposition and should be prominent in all materials. Client did not think the underscore on "And" was impactful enough in our last round.

4. Client wants to test use of QR Codes in all visual media. Believes most brands make a big mistake by making the QR Code too small. (Let's not make this mistake!)

5. Stay away from words like "production", "factory", "children",

"fatalities" as these may evoke negative cognitive links to our ongoing Philippines problem.

6. Everything needs to work seamlessly with our "Summer Season of Savings" sales event. This is our biggest sales driver of the year. This event needs to ROCK!

ADVERTISING IS LIKE EXERCISE.

Here's what the ROI guys don't understand about advertising. They think you can advertise today and measure the results tomorrow. It doesn't work that way.

If you're not used to running, and you run 5 miles today, you will not be stronger or healthier or feel better tomorrow. As a matter of fact, you'll probably feel like crap.

But if you run 5 miles every day, next year you probably will be stronger, and healthier, and feel better.

That's also how advertising works.

If you advertise today, your business is not going to suddenly be successful tomorrow or next week. But if you advertise every day, next year your business probably will get better, and healthier, and stronger.

Why do you think a can of Coca-Cola is worth 25¢ more than a can of Safeway cola? It's not because of the Coke ad you saw last night or last week. It's the ones you've seen your entire life.

Notice I said "probably." There are no guarantees. Just like exercise, sometimes advertising backfires. You can take off on a 5 mile run and have a heart attack after 10 minutes. Or you could run all year and wind up with a gimpy knee. You never know.

Similarly, you could advertise for a year and end up with nothing but a one-way ticket to the unemployment office. It's all about likelihoods and probabilities.

If you look at the leading brands in mainstream categories, the likelihood is that they have one thing in common — they advertise, and they do it a lot.

Does this mean that in all categories advertising is a surefire road to success? No.

But absence of it is a pretty reliable road to failure.

WHY INTERACTIVITY MAKES ADVERTISING LESS EFFECTIVE

The advertising and marketing industries had a dream. The dream was that interactive media would revolutionize advertising and make it far more relevant and effective.

There's only one problem. Consumers have shown no interest in interacting with advertising.

In fact, if people can easily interact with a medium they overwhelmingly do so to avoid advertising, not connect with it.

Click through rates on display ads continue to drop and are now below one in a thousand. Every attempt at interactive TV has been a dismal failure.

What marketers still refuse to comprehend is that, at best, advertising is a minor annoyance. It is pretty clear that most consumers are willing to go to substantial lengths to avoid it. Which makes the ability to interact with a medium the enemy of advertising.

This is nothing new. Radio advertising became less effective with the invention of the push-button car dial. TV advertising became less effective with the invention of the remote. TV spots were a lot more effective when you had to drag your ass off the couch to change the channel.

But there are a few exceptions to this. Happily there are some very talented people who can create ads that are so interesting, beautiful, or entertaining that people will not try to avoid them.

The other exception occurs when people are shopping. Someone actively looking for something is willing to connect.

These exceptions notwithstanding, easy interaction with a medium is not the advertiser's friend. But there is apparently no end to marketers' ability to delude themselves, and also no end to ad hustlers' willingness to feed these delusions.

The lovely fantasy of advertising interactivity has been undermined by an unfortunate fact of human nature — no one in his right mind volunteers for advertising.

HOW MANY COGNITIVE ANTHROPOLOGISTS
DOES IT TAKE TO MAKE A TV SPOT?

An agency just broke two new TV spots for Applebee's. This post is not about the spots. It's about the credits for the spots. Apparently it took more people to create this thing than *Gone With The Wind.* Below are the credits for the two spots which I found in an advertising trade publication:

Worldwide Chief Creative Officer: Rob Reilly

VPs, Executive Creative Directors: Steve Babcock, Mark Taylor

VP, Creative Director: Allen Richardson

Creative Directors: Dave Swartz, Scott MacGregor

Associate Creative Directors: Rich Ford, Brandt Lewis

Senior Art Director: David Gonsalves

Integrated Head of Video: Chad Hopenwasser

Senior Integrated Producer: Aaron Kovan

Integrated Producer: Annie Turlay

Food Shoot Production Company: MJZ

Food Shoot Director: Irv Blitz

Executive Producer: Franny Freiberger

Production Supervisor: Sabrina Mossberg

Live-Action Production Company: Moxie Pictures

Live-Action Director: Jared Hess

Executive Producers: Robert Fernandez, Lizzie Schwartz

Head of Production, Producer: Roger Zorovich

Line Producer: Laura Heflin

Director of Photography: Dariusz Wolskio

Postproduction: Plus Productions

VP, Executive Producer: Idalia Deshon

Integrated Producer: Andrea Krichevsky

Editor: Logan Hefflefinger

Assistant Editors: Chancler Haynes, Chadwick Schultz

VFX Artist: Adam Nix

Finishing Company: Method Studios
Executive Producer: Robert Owens
Music Company: JSM
Executive Integrated Music Producer: Bill Meadows Composers,
    Arrangers: Joel Simon, Jordan Lieb
Sound Design, Mix Company: Lime Studios
Sound Designer: Sam Casas
Assistant Sound Designer: Matthew Miller
Animation Company: Buck
Visual Effects Company: Method Studios
Visual Effects Editor: Claus Hansen
Assistant Visual Effects Editor: Krysten Richardson
Visual Effects Producer: Colin Clarry
EVP, Group Account Director: Danielle Whalen
VP, Account Director: Scott Sibley
Content Management Supervisor: Ted Morse
Content Supervisor: Greg Paige
Content Manager: Derek Effinger
Assistant Content Manager: Alex Kirk
Business Affairs: Lisa Gillies
Talent Consultant: Michelle Thompson
Cognitive Anthropologists: Andrew Teagle, Kaylin Goldstein,
    Amelia Hall
Traffic Manager: Megan O'Rourke

This gig had seven Creative Directors and four Content Managers. Hard to see how they managed to scrape by with only three Cognitive Anthropologists.

BULLETIN: AGENCY PEOPLE ARE UNHAPPY

Recently, Digiday ran a piece called *"Why Agency People Are Unhappy."*

Before we discuss how they got it all wrong, let's get a little perspective. Unhappy agency people are nothing new. Agency people are whiners, always have been and always will be. Many are lovable whiners, but whiners nonetheless.

Half of the whining is legitimate — many jobs in advertising suck.

Half of it is just the discontentment of people who consider themselves too good for what they are asked to do.

And the third half is the natural inclination of everyone everywhere to bitch and moan.

Now back to Digiday.

Has the level of discontentment in advertising gone up in recent years? My sense is that it has, substantially. While I've heard an incessant drumbeat of unhappiness among ad people for 4 decades, I believe it is now worse than ever.

Digiday drags out all the usual suspects to explain this:

- Demanding clients
- Low pay
- Horrendous hours
- Disrespect for the contribution
- Disrespect for creative work
- The effect of the Internet
- Fear of innovation

As far as I'm concerned, these are mostly effects. They are not the cause. The deeper cause of all this increased angst is something more subtle and misunderstood — it is the consolidation of the ad industry.

When I started in advertising, the largest agency in the U.S. was Y&R with about a 1.5% share of market. According to the latest figures I've seen, four enormous holding companies now control over 70% of the advertising in the U.S.

The advertising industry is, structurally, a totally different industry than it was when it was pleasanter and creative-er. It is also totally different culturally. This makes an enormous difference.

A handful of giant megaliths — controlled by financiers, accountants, lawyers and corporate flat tires (what a colleague of mine used to call "fearsomely dull men in grey suits") — run the ad industry. They are a very different breed from the craftspeople / entrepreneurs who built it.

I think you will find that the agencies in which people are most satisfied these days are either the independent agencies or the agencies that are so creatively successful that their holding company masters wouldn't dare mess with them.

There is no secret about what happens to most industries when they become consolidated — the customers become angry and the employees become dispirited. Look at the airline industry, the telecom industry, and the banking industry.

The ad industry will never be any different as long as it is controlled by the likes of Michael Roth and Martin Sorrell.

We sold our industry to the highest bidders. And in doing so, we sold our soul.

It's hard to be happy when you're soul-free.

AN INDUSTRY OF UMPIRES

In baseball, the players play the game and the umpires make sure there is a smooth and decorous process.

The fans come to see the talent of the players. When umpires impose themselves disproportionately on the flow of the game they are roundly booed.

The best umpires are the ones who are virtually invisible. The worst umpires are the ones who think the game is about them.

A very strange phenomenon has happened in the advertising industry. Almost unnoticed, the umpires have taken over the game.

The players — the people who actually make the ads — have been marginalized. They are now "support."

The business is in such a state of disarray that the umpires are playing the game. The account managers, the planners, the strategists and data analysts are now taking the at-bats and running the bases.

There has always been a certain type of activist "umpire" in the ad business. Like in baseball, the really good ones are catalysts for a smoother, more enjoyable and better played game. The really bad ones think the game is about them.

The sad thing is that while baseball fans would never pay to watch umpires play ball, clients seem to be comfortable with this arrangement.

Something has gone very wrong. Either the players no longer have the talent to keep the paying customers interested, or the customers have forgotten what the game is about.

ANALYZING EVERYTHING AND UNDERSTANDING NOTHING

Sometime in the near future advertising pundits will look back at the current era and reach the conclusion that we blew it.

They'll say we were focused on everything but the problem.

We had dashboards and metrics and click-throughs and webisodes and branded entertainment and a whole galaxy of new and used media outlets...but what we didn't have was very good advertising.

It seems silly to have to say this but our industry has reached a point of such grotesque confusion that I'm going to say it anyway — the business of advertising is advertising.

If the advertising isn't very good, what difference does the rest of it make?

We analyze everything and understand nothing.

We have forgotten that some of the best advertising ideas weren't the result of algorithms and analyses. They were the result of someone sitting on the potty with a yellow pad and coming up with a great idea.

I'm not advocating throwing caution to the wind and doing whatever the hell sounds like fun, but I am saying that we need to temper our arrogant belief in our analytical abilities with the realization that there is a great deal about how advertising works that is about imagination, not facts.

Our clients may think they want dashboards and data, but what they really need is ideas.

The longer we stay focused on gee-whiz technologies and media gimmicks while our creative work languishes, the more our value to our clients will erode.

With all the startling innovations in communication, technology, and media, one would think that creative innovation would follow as a natural offshoot. But it hasn't. Creativity doesn't work that way. It has its own timetable and its own mind.

Let's not forget why we're here.

THE RESTAURANT FOR PEOPLE WHO DON'T LIKE FOOD

In my hometown of Oakland, California, there's a restaurant I hate. It's very chic and popular with a certain type of person – a person who likes restaurants, but doesn't like food.

Everything about it is unappetizing. It has a cheerless austerity that appeals to the guilty wealthy. The food is very artfully arranged twigs and pebbles. It's as if the chef learned his craft working with Tinker Toys.

They are afraid to use any ingredient that might add flavor to one of their precious concoctions as it might also taint its virtue.

Today we have agencies like this. They are agencies for people who don't like advertising.

They are post-advertising agencies. They have no interest in the art, no passion for the craft.

They have no zeal for selling. They tell us that today's human does not want to be sold to. As if any human ever did.

They want to co-create, and have conversations, and share values.

Everything about these agencies is unappetizing. They, too, have a cheerless austerity. They believe that persuasion is an insult to their relationship with the consumer. They believe that selling will taint their virtue. They are bloodless, timid, and unenthusiastic.

Not me. I like selling. I like persuasion. I like advertising. I like food.

Chapter Three:

Get Off My Lawn

BEWARE OF MARKETERS WITH IDEOLOGIES

In 1996, bestselling author Seth Godin had this to say to Fast Company... *"I guarantee you that by the year 2000, Internet banner ads will be gone."* Oops.

Let's be fair to Seth. He's a very smart guy and he has been right about a lot of things. But the problem with the above statement, like so many aspects of marketing these days, is that it is rooted in ideology.

Seth's ideology was "permission marketing." He believed that the "interruption model" of traditional advertising was on the way out, and that in order to communicate effectively with consumers, marketers would need their "permission."

Like much of new age marketing philosophy, it sounds lovely. The problem is that the world is impossibly complicated. Having operating principles is fine, but being ideologically committed to a "big idea" often ends in a train wreck.

Ideology is often the downfall of pundits, historians and marketers. Philip Tetlock is an author and professor at the University of California-Berkeley. He's the winner of lots of impressive awards — and an expert on experts.

According to Tetlock, experts who are most often wrong are those who have an ideological commitment to a "big idea."

"They tended to have one big, beautiful idea that they loved to stretch, sometimes to the breaking point. They tended to be articulate and very persuasive as to why their idea explained everything. The media often love (them.)"

People attached to ideologies often are not able to adapt their "big, beautiful idea" to the constant surprises of the real world. Instead, they re-interpret the real world to fit their big, beautiful idea.

In fact, what has happened is that contrary to permission model theory, the interruption model is becoming more dominant on the web, not less.

Facebook is now chock-a-block with display ads and sponsored posts.

Every news and entertainment site is packed with pre-roll. Interstitial ads drive us all crazy every time we click to a new site. Meanwhile, permission marketing is useful but limited. It mainly allows us to preach to the converted. It may be beneficial for popular, high interest products and categories. But for the average business - a maker of vacuum cleaner bags or pencils or mufflers - it offers little in the way of leverage.

In the article quoted above, Godin also went on to say... *"Marketing is a contest for people's attention."*

He is certainly right about this. However, the grand visions and big, beautiful new ideas about marketing that were supposed to help us gain people's attention in new ways, have proven disappointingly hollow. The result is that banner advertising — that horrible, corrupt, and maligned old thing — not only is not "gone," it is metastasizing.

Many of us wish that banner ads had disappeared in 2000, as Seth promised. But one of the lessons about advertising is that practicality consistently outperforms ideology.

THE 6 STAGES OF DIGITAL DELUSION

In today's world of marketing, delusional thinking is not just acceptable, it's mandatory.

Digital media have been the primary cause and the primary beneficiary of delusional thinking. The fascinating thing is that the cycle of delusion has been going on for over 15 years and we still don't recognize it. Here are the 6 stages of digital delusion:

1. *The Miracle Is Acknowledged:* It may be podcasting or banner advertising, YouTube, The Ice Bucket Challenge, or Big Data. Whatever it is, it is going to "change everything." It will be the focus of hysterical attention in the trade press and will often find its way into the business section of the newspaper.

2. *The Big Success:* A company somewhere has a big success with it. This is where the danger starts. The success is plastered all over every trade magazine and analyzed at every conference. It is "proof " that the miracle is real.

3. *Experts Are Hatched:* Clever entrepreneurs gather up a Powerpointful of cliches and march them around from conference to conference. They write articles, and even books, on how not to be left behind.

4. *The Bandwagon Rolls:* Everyone who knows nothing is suddenly asking the marketing department, "what is our (*the new miracle*) strategy?" Fearing that she will be thought insufficiently trendy, every CMO is suddenly looking for an agency that is expert at (*the new miracle*).

5. *Reality Rears Its Ugly Head:* The numbers dribble in. Oops... people are ignoring our miracle by the millions. The miracle seems to be working for everyone but us!

6. *The Back-Pedaling Begins:* "Well, it's just part of an integrated program..." say the former zealots. The experts start blaming the victims, "Hey, we never promised...We told you you had to..."

This cycle has repeated itself so many times that it is comical.

Here are just some of the digital miracles that have turned out to be "just part of an integrated program" — blogs... podcasts... MySpace... Second Life... widgets...YouTube... Facebook apps...Twitter... iAds...FourSquare...QR codes... and now... who the hell knows.

Meet the new boss. Same as the old boss.

THE DUMBEST CLIENT I EVER DIDN'T GET

During my career in advertising I had the pleasure of meeting hundreds of nice, intelligent people. And more than a few real nitwits.

Among the nitwits, one stands out.

Thankfully, he never became a client. As a matter of fact, I only had the pleasure of being with him in one meeting. But in that one meeting it became clear to me that a well-dressed, well-spoken, *internationally* handsome imbecile could really go far in marketing.

I don't want to embarrass anybody, so I won't get too specific.

One of our clients, a very successful food company here in the U.S., was doing a joint venture with a European company to introduce a new "fresh fruit" product. Well, it was *kind of* fresh and *kind of* fruit, but nonetheless, it was positioned as a "fresh fruit" product. It was juice-like.

The product was just so-so and if everything went perfectly I gave it about a 30% chance of success. For some reason the introduction in the U.S. was being handled by the cmo of the European partner, which gives you some idea of how well thought-out this whole enterprise was.

We were finalists in a multi-agency circle jerk. To the European cmo we were just some dumb agency from San Francisco. He was used to *internationally* dumb agencies.

At the final presentations, he came down from the mountain to attend the meetings. We did a good presentation — nothing brilliant, but solid and workable and capable of creating a successful launch.

And then Mr. Euromoron stepped in and revealed his brilliant strategy:

"Do you know how many people in the U.S. never buy fresh fruit juice?" he asked rhetorically. "Almost 50%!"

"Really?" I replied. *And so...?*

"So that means half the people in the U.S. are the perfect target for our new product."

Hold it, you're not saying....

"We're going to target all those people who are *not* buying fruit juice and..."

"Excuse me," I said. "You mean you are *not* going to target a juice product to people who *buy* juice? You want to target it to the people who *don't*?"

"Yes," he said, with the pride of those who believe they are thinking 'outside the box' but are really thinking inside their ass. "Look at the enormous opportunity."

"May I ask a question?" I asked. "Why do you think these people don't buy fruit juice?"

"Because... *some bullshit about convenience.... or some other bullshit about marketing... or some more bullshit about engagement....*" he replied.

"No, *you fucking moron*, it's because *they don't fucking like it, you stupid fuck.*" Is what I wanted to say.

But being the gentleman that I am, I just farted and left the room.

Oh, we didn't get the account and the product died in about 10 minutes.

WEB LITTER: NOW IT'S CONTENT

The dismal record of online advertising has caused a minor crisis among the thousands of agencies who make a living creating the stuff.

It is getting difficult for them to convince anyone that blogs or podcasts or social media are the marketing miracles they were once purported to be. No one is that stupid anymore. I mean, except the odd CMO.

So the folks who create all this web debris have had to look for some new magic to sell. That miracle is called "content."

Content isn't a new thing. But it is enjoying a new life. You see, all the specific things that the web promoters promised us would be magic have turned out to be a lot less than promised. So they've renamed it all "content" because it is non-specific — no one knows what the hell it is. And if you don't know what it is, how can you criticize it?

What exactly is content, you ask? Well, it seems that as long as you can upload it, and it's not an ad, it's "content."

So all that online detritus that no one pays any attention to, the blogs and podcasts and billions of "user generated" videos and corporate Facebook pages, now have a new life. They are now "content." Previously they were just litter blowing unnoticed through the dark, dusty corridors of the web. But now that they have been re-branded as "content" they are once again awesome.

"Content" is a word that helps web promoters hide what they are doing. They do not say they are creating a newsletter, or a recipe, or an e-mail, or a post, or a web site, or a game — they say they are creating "content." It's so much more enchanting (and marketable.)

Posting an online recipe may be useful to a food marketer, but calling it "content" is just pretentious drivel. It's a damn recipe.

The idea that "content" as a concept is an important marketing discipline is absurd. An old pizza crust is garbage. But an uploaded *picture* of an old pizza crust is "content."

By invoking the c-word they are doing what marketing people do best — avoiding the specific and hiding behind jargon.

How, you may ask, did things that were clearly unproductive become awesome again? To understand this you have to understand the mind of the web zealot. The web zealot's marketing mind is very imaginative. It cares about high-minded issues. In fact, a marketing activity without a noble purpose — for example TV advertising — makes no sense to this person. The fact that TV ads are stupid and annoying is all he can see. The fact that they actually fucking work is of no interest. Without a noble purpose they cannot be taken seriously.

Back before all the underachieving online activities became "content" they were supposed to sell something. This is anathema to the web marketing mind. Now that they are content, they are no longer *allowed* to sell anything. From the Content Marketing Institute:

> *"Basically, content marketing is the art of communicating with your customers and prospects without selling. It is non-interruption marketing. Instead of pitching your products or services, you are delivering information that makes your buyer more intelligent."*

Yeah, that's what the public is waiting for — the marketing industry to make them more intelligent.

Content, it's been said, is a demonstration of your like-mindedness with your customer. It shows that you have a "shared purpose" with her. It is a "utility" and is "compelling" and provides the consumer with "value." It is helpful and fascinating and because your customer appreciates it so much she will engage with your brand and become a huge fan of your company.

Sounds lovely, doesn't it? This is the just the kind of virtuous philosophy that the web marketing mind can really embrace. There's just one little problem. It's all bullshit.

According to the most recent data I could find, Google says that as of July of last year, there were 38 *trillion* pages on the web. Every page is "content." And each page may have several individual items of content. For example, on your Facebook page every update is new content. So is every little ad. So is every comment and every photo.

How much total "content" is there on the web? Who the hell knows? But for the sake of simplicity, let's just stick with Google's 38 trillion number.

Now let's go to the blackboard. If a person were to do nothing her entire life — no eating, no sleeping, no getting high — but surf the web for "content" in 1 minute increments, it will take her 72 million years to get around to the average page of content.

And if your content is below average...gosh, it could take a long time.

HERE'S TO THE BOBBLEHEADS

Here's to the bobbleheads.

Here's to the ones who sit at every meeting and nod in agreement.

Here's to the ones who never have a dangerous idea or an interesting opinion.

Here's to the ones who always agree with the highest ranking person in the room.

Here's to the ones who go to conferences and tweet out the banalities.

Here's to the guys and gals who start every sentence with, "The client said…"

Here's to the ones who think their job is to make someone happy.

Here's to the ones who can't finish a sentence without saying "disrupt" or "engage."

Here's to the ones who have no questions.

Here's to the ones who agree with the last person they spoke to.

Here's to the ones who produce the biggest decks and the fuzziest briefs.

Here's to the ones who know all of the platitudes and none of the facts.

Here's to the true believers — the new kings and queens of the ad industry.

Here's to the bobbleheads!

THE DANGER IN BEING DIFFERENT

In advertising everyone is faking it.

I mean *everyone*— you, me, your boss, your client, Martin Sorrell — everyone.

Let me be even clearer: Nobody knows a fucking thing about how any of this works. We throw money at it and we cross our fingers.

Having said that, it is also true that there are some people with exceptional instincts. These people are very good at "precision guessing." That is, they are much better at *intuiting what is going to work* than the average ad bozo.

These are the stars in our industry. While I have met a number of good precision guessers, the best ones I have met in advertising have been creatives.

They hide their exceptional intuition behind the language of marketing — strategy and benefits and brand personality and all the other bullshit jargon of our trade. But make no mistake about it — they are cleverly using our language to bamboozle us. They are going on their instincts but employing our vocabulary to pretend they are one of us.

In other words, they solve the problem viscerally and then reverse engineer a rationale that we can accept.

This is a very good thing. If they told the truth— that they are just making shit up — no one would listen to them.

But let's get back to the rest of us for a minute.

Recently, Forrester Research released a report saying that social media marketing on Facebook and Twitter is substantially worthless. This is a conclusion some of us reached years ago.

When I left the agency business, people within agencies were essentially forbidden from saying this. If you did, you were labeled a Luddite, a dinosaur, or just plain stupid. You "didn't get it." It was a one-way ticket out the door.

Sadly, the consequences of being considered out of step are far more powerful than the satisfaction of finding out you were right five years later.

When nobody knows anything — like about social media, for example — you would think that unconventional opinions would be numerous and welcome. In fact, it is just the opposite.

Ignorance demands conformity. Because everyone knows they are faking it, they seek comfort in the warmth of consensus.

Speaking out against the agreed-upon fantasy is looked at as both heresy and betrayal. No one is more despised or vilified than the nonbeliever in a tenuous theology.

And so the people who knew better about social media — the precision guessers — were coerced into shutting up. Agencies were making money, careers were being built, conferences were being held, clients were demanding more of the magic.

The lesson is clear: When everyone is faking it in unison, there is danger in being different.

TIME FOR SORRELL TO GO

There is a small group of men who have ruined the advertising industry.

They have made it leaner and meaner. They have made it more efficient. They have made it more productive. They have squeezed all the fat out of it. They have also squeezed all the life out of it.

They have replaced ideas with data. They have replaced value with efficiency.

They are accountants and investors and financial wise guys. The one thing they are not is advertising people.

Advertising was once an industry of craftsmen and craftswomen. Industrious people would start their own agencies. There were dozens of independent, entrepreneurial agencies in every major city. Now there are a handful of advertising holding companies that run the world.

The advertising business has been consolidated into submission. As Dave Trott says, we have become an industry of bank managers. Martin Sorrell, CEO of WPP, the world's largest advertising agency holding company, gave a talk in London recently. According to website The Drum, he told the attendees...

'The medium, or media, has become "more important" than the message...'

This is the grotesque outlook of a publisher who thinks the paper is more important than the writing. It is the delusion of an impresario who thinks the instruments are more important than the music. It is the chirping of a philistine who thinks the paint is more valuable than the artwork.

This is not acceptable. Sorrell and his clones who head up other agency holding companies need to find new industries to rape. They have been a massive, tragic failure. They have enriched themselves and impoverished an industry.

It's time for these people to go.

AD INDUSTRY IS THE WEB'S LAPDOG

One of the important responsibilities of the advertising industry is to be an "honest broker" between our clients and the media. We have failed miserably.

While we have been aggressive about detailing the woes of traditional media — the decline of the newspaper business; the problems of radio; the movement away from broadcast television — we have glossed over or completely ignored the shortcomings of the web. We have failed to educate our clients on the serious deficiencies related to web advertising:

-62% of web traffic is reportedly phony

-54% of display ads paid for reportedly never ran

-57% of video ads paid for are apparently never seen

-Fraud and corruption are massive and reportedly in the billions

-Interaction with display advertising is essentially non-existent

-As much as half of all video viewed on line may be porn

-Regardless of what media buyers say, nobody knows where their online ads run

It is clear why the ad industry has been complicit with online media in covering up these issues — the web has become a gold mine for agencies.

WPP, the world's largest agency network, currently derives about 1/3 of its revenue of $16 billion from digital work and is aiming for 45% to come from the web within a few years.

Not only is income from digital sources rising, smart agencies have discovered how to squeeze more profit from this income than from traditional advertising.

For one thing, online work is never done. A website is never finished, a social media or content program always needs feeding, and display advertising always needs optimizing. If you're charging by the hour — and your profit is built into your hourly rate — more work always means more profit.

But when you're doing traditional work and you're on a monthly retainer or fee, more work means less profit.

The ad industry has become the web's lapdog — exaggerating the effectiveness of social media marketing, ignoring the abominable click-through rates of "interactive" advertising, glossing over the fraud and corruption, and becoming a de facto sales arm for the online ad industry.

Self-interest has come into conflict with responsibility. Guess what's winning?

HOW DO YOU UNTRAIN A GENERATION?

For almost two thousand years, up until the late 19th century, one of the most common treatments for illness was bloodletting.

Medical practitioners, who were trained in the practice of bloodletting, never questioned its efficacy. They just assumed it worked because they were taught it worked and they credulously attributed the fact that some people got well to the treatment.

We are faced with a similar problem today in advertising. We have a whole generation of people who have been taught nonsense. They are now in important positions in marketing and advertising, and they are practicing what they have been taught.

For almost 20 years, advertising programs, marketing courses, and professional development classes have taught these people principles that can now be labeled either seriously flawed or outright baloney. Some of them are:

- Consumers want to interact with advertising.
- The "interruption" model is dead, and the "permission" model is transcendent.
- Consumers want to have "relationships" with brands and be "engaged" with them.
- Consumers are heavily influenced by online "conversations about brands."
- Broadcast media are "dead."

People who were taught these fictions are now CMOs, creative directors, and brand managers. They are running the marketing world and they will continue to do so for a good long time.

Marketing and advertising have always had their share of questionable beliefs. But never before in my experience has a whole generation of marketing and advertising people been taught an entire set of principles that is so lacking in a factual basis, and so influenced by anecdotes and fantasies.

In fact,

- Consumer interaction with online advertising is essentially nonexistent. The average click rate of banner ads is 8 in 10,000.
- The "interruption" model of advertising is kicking the ass of the "permission" model. Take a look at your Facebook page. It is swimming in traditional, paid ads.
- Consumer engagement with Facebook posts is 7 in 10,000. With Twitter posts it is 3 in 10,000. And this is among a brands *fans*!
- Online "conversations" about brands are a marketing delusion. Once again, have a look at your Facebook page or your Twitter feed.
- As I write this, 96% of video is viewed on a television. 4% is viewed on line.

Paradoxically, a generation that has been raised to worship data, is ignorant of the data that has evolved to demonstrate the fundamental fallacies of their principles.

Worse, they dismiss those of us who question their "bloodletting" as ignorant heretics.

Chapter Four:

Advice You Never Asked For

WHATEVER YOU DO, DON'T BE YOURSELF

If you want to be successful in marketingland, one of the first things you have to learn is to ignore all the baloney about "being yourself." As a matter of fact, at all costs, *do not* be yourself.

Being yourself is a one-way ticket to Starbucksville.

I don't know who you are, or what "yourself " is like, but I guarantee you, "yourself " will be a big flop in marketingworld.

In marketingworld, you are expected to talk like this:

> *"(White Castle) is a beloved challenger brand...They seek an agency partner to align with their idea-rich, entrepreneurial culture and evolve the brand's cultural relevance, especially among the millennial target."*

See what I mean? That's an actual quote from an actual consultant. I don't care how full of shit "yourself " is, yourself can't be *that* full of shit.

Yourself might have said:

> *"White Castle is a bottom-feeding purveyor of unspeakable crap that just got a new CMO who wants an agency that will kiss his ass."*

But I'm afraid that just wouldn't sit well with the new masters of marketing. That's why, to be successful in marketing, you have to be very careful not to be yourself.

Here are some simple rules to follow to keep from being yourself:

- Do not speak in simple declarative sentences
- Do not express doubts about anything
- Do not tell your colleagues what pathetic kiss-asses they are
- Never disagree with the highest ranking person in the room
- When a superior says the stupidest fucking thing you've ever heard, smile and nod

- Remember, every sentence you speak or write must contain
  the word "brand" or "engagement"

I'm afraid that being yourself simply will not align with marketing's idea-rich entrepreneurial culture or evolve your cultural relevance especially among the millennial target.

So take my advice, amigo. Be the other guy. Okay, now get out there and knock 'em dead.

3 WAYS TO NEVER BE WRONG

One of the big problems with being a marketing expert is that deep down you know that you really don't know anything. If you knew something, you'd be rolling in money from all your marketing brilliance. It's that "those who can, do..." thing.

Most of the time it doesn't matter. You can get away with not knowing anything by talking in riddles, parables, and indecipherable jargon. For example, here are three points from an article I read recently:

- *"Notification windows introduce a thin layer for rapid engagement."*
- *"The Internet of Things is a hot and beautiful mess until it becomes the Internet of Everything"*
- *"Mass personalization and full funnel marketing suites reset vendor landscape and change how brands "think" and work."*

Maybe there's something in there that means something, but I'll be fucked if I know what it is. Nonetheless, the article was read by hundreds of thousands of people who are apparently a lot smarter than I am. It received thousands of "thumbs ups."

I guess as long as you write stuff like that and avoid real English you'll be fine. People, being the insecure dimwits they are, assume that since you're an expert and they're not, all this hogwash must mean something.

The tough part comes when you have to say something in *real* English with *real* words and *real* meaning. Because if you're a proto-typical marketing professional pretty much everything you say has already been said a thousand times and is going to turn out to be wrong.

Consequently, you need a strategy for dealing with those unfortunate times when you can't speak in nursery rhymes and have to actually say something.

Here are three effective strategies for being dead wrong, but maintaining your "expert" status.

- *"I wasn't wrong, I was ahead of my time."* This is also known as the "just wait, you'll see" defense.
- *"Of course, I didn't mean it literally."* You see, the philistines don't understand the subtleties of an allegory.
- *"It may seem like I was wrong, but if you look beyond…"* This is the "broader view" defense and is sometimes known as "torturing the logic."

Fortunately, most people's hair is on fire 90% of the time and they are too distracted to go back and see how wrong you were. But just in case you run into some pain-in-the-ass who is insistent on pointing out your imperfections, keep these three defenses in mind and you'll be just fine.

THROWING COLD WATER ON THE ICE BUCKET

One of the dependable characteristics of dumb guys is the attribution of far-reaching meaning to random occurrences.

In the past, people thought lightning was an expression of godly anger. Comets and meteors were thought to augur the end of the world.

You can always tell who the half-bright marketing promoters are because they, too, attribute deep meaning to every random marketing phenomenon.

As soon as something comes out of nowhere to be a marketing success, they get busy developing a big dumb interpretation of it and drawing specious conclusions. They produce long-winded essays and blog posts about the lessons we fools should learn from the miracle.

Perhaps you remember "The Blair Witch Project." It was a movie that out-of-the-blue became a huge success driven by a small online advertising campaign. All the half-wit marketing gurus saw this as a seismic shift in movie marketing that would forever end the practice of spending large sums on traditional advertising by movie studios. Of course, it did no such thing and studios are spending more than ever to market their films.

Then there was Zappos. Its unlikely success was interpreted as a signal of the beginning of a new age in which enormous business goals would be achieved with just a little clever Tweetage. Once again, Zappos turned out to be an anomaly that no one has been able to duplicate.

Then there was the Arab Spring in which communications experts explained to us how social media had become the indomitable force for political change that was going to bring freedom, democracy, and kale smoothies to the Middle East. Yeah, any day now.

And now we have the Ice Bucket Challenge.

Every dim bulb is drawing grand conclusions from this one-off. I guarantee you there are about a thousand Powerpoint presentations currently in the works explaining the "Five Critical Lessons" we should be learning from it.

In fact, there is only one lesson to be learned from the Ice Bucket Challenge: sometimes silly shit catches on.

THE VIEW FROM NOWHERE

I am often criticized by those who don't agree with my incautious opinions about the direction of our industry. That's fine. After a while, I don't agree with some of the things I write myself.

But there is one line of criticism that I find truly annoying.

It is the idea that I am an old "traditional" ad guy and therefore I don't "get it." The essence of the argument is that my views are tainted by my age and history.

My views are certainly *influenced* by my history. Anyone who is not influenced by experience is an idiot. That is different, however, from being tainted.

What these critics don't seem to understand is that there is no "view from nowhere."

Everyone's opinions are shaped by their circumstances — digital zealots no less than old traditional ad people. Their criticism implies that the only valid opinions are those of people who are a blank slate. It assumes that there are people who appeared on earth immaculately (okay, maybe there was one) and whose opinions are free of history and experience.

This is not the basis for serious debate. However, it is the only line of defense for people who can't argue on merit.

Since there is no view from nowhere, perhaps the people whose opinions we should value most are those with a "view from everywhere." Those who have seen it all, done it all, and are in a position to provide a reliable narration.

While I certainly do not have a "view from everywhere," I have seen the marketing and agency businesses from a lot of angles. I started on the client side, I became an agency copywriter, graduated to creative director, ran an agency, worked as ceo of a global agency in the US, started a new agency, did both traditional and digital advertising, and have had a degree of success as a social media "brand."

My opinions may be dead wrong. But the criticism that they are tainted because I started as a "traditional ad guy" is as stupid as criticizing a baseball manager because he started as a player.

I know you don't give a shit about this self-serving twaddle, but I needed to get it off my chest.

SEX AND COMMERCE

Back in high school there were people who were "heavy users" of sex. Remember them?

They often had one characteristic in common — they were promiscuous.

They didn't just have lots of sex with one person. As we used to say, they "got around."

The world of commerce is like that, too. Heavy users in a category tend to be promiscuous. They tend to try lots of different brands in a category. They get around.

In his book *How Brands Grow*, Prof. Byron Sharp gives a good example of this. Someone who is a heavy user in the fast food category might go to McDonald's 4 out of 10 times; Subway 2.5 in 10; Wendy's 1.5 in 10; Taco Bell 1 in 10...etc.

People in marketing often wrongly equate heavy usage with loyalty. They think that heavy users in a category tend to be brand loyal. And that heavy usage of a brand indicates brand loyalty.

The truth can be quite the opposite. In the above example, the heavy fast food user might also be a heavy user of McDonald's. He may go to McDonald's 4 times a week. But he is *not* brand loyal. In fact, most of the time (6 out of 10) he patronizes a competitor.

This is true in many categories. Heavy users of sneakers (like yours truly) will tend to have Nikes, Adidas, and Reeboks in their closets. Heavy users of wine are very avid brand jumpers. Heavy travelers visit a lot of different locations. 72% of Pepsi drinkers also drink Coke.

Meanwhile, light users can be very brand loyal. My parents didn't eat out much, but when they did, they always went to the same places.

Of course, this does not mean there are no heavy category or brand users who are highly brand loyal. But in general, the idea that heavy users in a category or of a brand are more loyal than light users is not just mistaken, it is dangerous.

It's dangerous for two reasons. First, because it fosters the infantile fantasy that people care deeply about brands and want to have "relationships" with them.

Second, it has large implications for advertising strategy. Success of a brand is not uniquely related to high degrees of brand loyalty. Let me repeat that. Success of a brand is not uniquely related to high degrees of brand loyalty.

In fact, the most important success factor for mainstream consumer brands is not how many *loyal* customers you have, but how many *total* customers you have. Which is why the current obsession with "engagement" is so misguided.

The idea that your success is dependent upon your customers becoming deeply emotionally attached to your brand is a delusion. Consumers are promiscuous. Most successful brands have a customer profile that is a mile wide and an inch deep. They're just not that into you.

As Martin Weigel says... *"Your consumers are just someone else's consumers who occasionally buy you."*

That is also why the current mania for spending enormous amounts of time, money, and energy getting your "fans" to "engage" with you is such a silly preoccupation. Having your customers "like" you may be nice, but having your competitors' customers *try* you is what builds your business.

Wanna grow your brand? You don't need more engagement. You need more customers.

THE TECHNOLOGY TRAP

I have developed a rather distressing reputation as a Luddite dinosaur who hates technology. I may be a Luddite dinosaur, but I don't hate technology.

As a former science teacher I love science and technology and am a sucker for all kinds of tech gizmos that I probably don't need.

I have another distressing reputation as an apologist for the broadcast industry, particularly TV. Once again, I plead innocent. I don't own a TV station (I wish I did) and have no particular interest in the success or failure of the medium.

In fact, while Nielsen says the average American spends about 4 times as much time watching TV as he does online, I probably spend 10 times more time on line than I do watching television.

So why do I have these bad reputations? I think it's because I have a high regard for the difference between a fact and an opinion.

Most of what I read about the advantages that tech-based advertising (i.e., online advertising) has over traditional advertising seem to be opinions masquerading as facts. With the exception of search, I have read a lot of assertions, but very few facts that convince me that the web is an uncommonly powerful advertising medium. If anything, I have been convinced of the opposite.

Thus far it appears that most of the new technology-based advertising methodologies have delivered substantially less than promised.

There is no doubt that the traditional advertising world has its fill of questionable practices and gross inefficiencies. However, having been ceo of an ad agency that did both traditional and digital advertising, it seems to me we spent a lot more time "massaging" our online numbers than we ever had to do with TV numbers.

But the technology delusion goes deeper than just media. Technology voodoo is becoming the new marketing voodoo.

I used to warn my clients that marketing is not magic. It is not the answer to every problem. If your product is lousy, marketing can't fix that. If your location is lousy, marketing can't fix that. If your store is dirty, or your employees surly, or your business model screwed up, or your parking lot a mess, marketing can't fix that.

It seems to me that today the magical voodoo answer is no longer marketing, it has become technology. The truth is, unless you're in the tech business or you make machines or gadgets, consumers really don't care that much about technology.

Even when you get a technological advantage, it is usually very short-lived and soon turns into just another cost of doing business.

The construction guy who put the first flush toilet into the first home must have had a huge technological advantage — for a couple of months. Then everyone started doing it.

Go back 20 years. Having a website was seen as a giant asset. Companies who announced the launch of a website actually saw their stock prices go higher. Today announcing the launch of a website is greeted with as much excitement as changing the plants in the lobby.

I don't know which bank introduced online banking. But they must have thought they found a gold mine. Today, every bank has to have online banking and it probably costs them a fortune to maintain.

As new technology is adopted by everyone, what starts as a competitive advantage often quickly evolves into just another cost of doing business.

Because of my speaking gigs, I have the opportunity to attend many business conferences. It is remarkable to me how much time is spent on technology voodoo and how little time is spent on solving the real problems of real customers.

Most of the technology talk I hear is of the gee-whiz, jet-pack, moving-sidewalk variety that almost never comes to fruition. And if it does, it creates a giant QR-code yawn among consumers.

Technological improvements are nice. But they are not an instant fix for most business problems.

Technology seduces us into thinking we can solve our problems by spending money instead of changing behaviors. Which is about the most damaging trap a business can fall into.

7 SECRETS OF SUCCESSFUL LAZY ASS BUMS

I hate working.

I hate sitting in an office. I hate going to meetings. I hate writing performance reviews. I hate "nurturing" people. I hate listening to bullshit artists and know-nothing loudmouths who dominate the business world. Yet somehow I managed to have a reasonably successful career.

Here are my 7 secrets of success.

1. *Assume everyone is faking it.* Nobody knows a thing about advertising. All the rules are bullshit. There are a few people who can make good ads. That's all there is.

2. *Preparation is everything.* If you are not the best prepared person in every meeting you are just another empty t-shirt. You will never get your way and you will always be second rate.

3. *Do as little work as possible at the office.* Do your real work somewhere else. It's almost impossible to do anything useful in an office. Offices are for meetings and phone calls and memos and emails and Powerpoints and politics and bullshit.

4. *Worry about everything.* If you don't worry you don't care. Figure out what's going to go wrong and be prepared when it does.

5. *Stay as far away from big organizations as possible.* Corporations will suck all the joy out of your life and all the life out of your joy. Big corporations are poison, and the more they pay you the more they own you.

6. *Pay no attention to the industry.* The more you read about what other agencies or other clients are doing the more you're going to become a cliché spewing zombie. Advertising ain't that complicated. Figure it out for yourself.

7. *Be satisfied.* You don't have to work for the biggest agency in the world or be the best art director on the planet to be

successful and happy. You're not going to be Bill Bernbach anyway, so forget about it. If you're doing work that is respectable, and you're not suffering 90% of the time, you're way ahead of most of the poor bastards in this business. Enjoy it.

That's as close to a pep talk as I get.

Chapter Five:

Old And In The Way

WHY DO MARKETERS HATE OLD PEOPLE?

One of the most infamous advertising campaigns in the history of the auto industry was called, "This Is Not Your Father's Oldsmobile."

The premise was that Oldsmobile was suddenly a vehicle for young people. There were only three problems with this campaign:

1. Young people couldn't afford and didn't buy new cars
2. When they did, they'd rather stick a jelly donut up their ass than buy an Oldsmobile
3. The campaign insulted the people who did buy Oldsmobiles - their parents

Apparently, Oldsmobile thought it was a good idea to malign their real customers and flatter the people who would never buy their products. Why? Because their real customers were old, and everyone in advertising and marketing hates old people.

It may have been the first time in the history of business that a company told its best customers that its product was no longer for them.

Marketers, it seems, would rather pander fruitlessly to young people than make real money selling things to old people.

The idea of people over 50 driving their cars, drinking their coffee, eating their hamburgers, and wearing their sneakers is so appalling and such an embarrassment that marketers willfully ignore and disparage the most valuable economic group in the history of the world.

Well, believe it or not, the Oldsmobile campaign flopped, and ultimately Oldsmobile folded.

What hasn't folded, however, is marketers' irrational obsession with young people and disdain for old people.

Today, marketers are just as likely to target people simply because they are young — even though they have no money and cannot and will not buy their products.

Conversely, they are just as likely to ignore people who are old — even though they have lots of money and are prime targets for their products.

Marketers contempt for and prejudice against older people is a remarkable and fascinating story. They have volumes of data that tell them about the size and power of the over 50 market, but because of their hard-wired prejudices they are blind to it.

If you could find a group

> ...who was responsibly for about half of all consumer spending
>
> ...who control over 70% of all the wealth in the country
>
> ...who have about 80% of the savings
>
> ...who dominate 94% of all CPG categories
>
> ...who buy almost 2/3's of all new cars
>
> ...who own 57% of all second and vacation homes and all the stuff that goes with that
>
> ...who are far easier and cheaper to reach than other groups would you ignore them?

There is only one type of person confused enough to do that — a marketing person.

If we dropped marketing people in from the moon and they looked at the data, they would immediately understand how important it is to aim marketing activity at people over 50.

Unfortunately, our marketing leaders don't come from the moon. They come from New York and LA and Chicago where decades of prejudices and legends have overwhelmed simple, clear thinking.

I was speaking to a very smart ad agency guy recently. He made a great point: *"If I could talk to CFOs about this, they'd get it in 5 seconds. But I have to talk to CMOs."*

According to Nielsen, people over 50 are *"the most valuable generation in the history of marketing."* Yet only 5% of advertising is directed at them.

Why? Because marketers are embarrassed by them. They are

afraid that 18-year-olds will, god forbid, see people over 50 using their products.

Marketers think that people over 50 are decrepit old farts. Marketers cannot understand that Barack Obama, Jerry Seinfeld, Condoleezza Rice, Bruce Springsteen, Meryl Streep and tens of millions of others are all over 50. They are healthy, wealthy, and wise. And, in many ways, hipper and more youthful than the marketers.

Oh, but they're dying out, right? Not exactly. Between now and 2030 the population over 50 will grow at about three times the rate of adults under 50.

Marketers are also under the delusion that older people want to be like young people. Yeah, Steven Spielberg is aching to be like Justin Bieber, and Michelle Obama is just itching to be like the doofuses in Taco Bell commercials.

But let's say these folks are right and older people want to be just like young people. That is still no reason to *target* young people. Showing young people in an ad is one thing, but for many brands targeting young people makes no sense at all.

As a former ad guy, I am sorry to say that too many people in marketing and advertising are obsessed with people like themselves. They think that everyone is a young, big city, coastal hipster.

Despite their pretensions of leading-edge hipness, they are mired in beliefs and practices that are 30 years out of date.

THE POLLUTED FOUNTAIN OF YOUTH

Anyone who's ever had a parent knows one thing for sure: Old people think young people are idiots.

If you're young, your parents hate your music, hate your haircut, hate your friends, hate your language, hate your clothing... it's an inviolable rule of nature.

This is nothing new. It's been going on for generations. Ever since youth culture emerged as a social phenomenon, every generation of parents has thought that every generation of kids were a bunch of bozos.

The only people who don't seem to know this are us advertising people. According to us, older people don't just admire young people, they long to be like them.

It's no coincidence that people in the ad industry tend to be young. All this youth worship is really just narcissism masquerading as business strategy.

What our agency masterminds don't seem to understand is that there is a difference between wanting to be *youthful,* and wanting to be *like young people.*

People of a certain age certainly want to be youthful. But their idea of being youthful is being like they were 15 years ago. Not being like young people are now.

Now that people over 50 are dominating our economy, it's about time agencies (and marketers) learned to draw a distinction. There's a difference between wanting to be youthful and wanting to be like young people. Ask your parents.

NOBODY LEARNS ANYTHING

The very first post I wrote for this blog almost 8 years ago was called *Aiming Low* and was about marketers' obsession with targeting young people in advertising.

A few months later I wrote a piece about Pontiac mindlessly doing exactly that: "According to Ad Age, Pontiac is shifting its advertising efforts toward media that appeal to younger audiences such as video game tie-ins, Web ads and spots on sports channels and late-night shows."

The logic of this is perfectly dumb and, as such, perfectly in line with the reflexes of so many marketers... A few facts:

1. The average Pontiac buyer was over 50.
2. Baby Boomers and older comprised over 60% of the market for new cars.
3. Of the 13 cars the average American will buy in a lifetime, 8 will be bought after they're 50.
4. Even if they wanted a Pontiac (which they didn't and never would) young people can't afford new cars, and no lender in his right mind will finance them.

Now that Pontiac is dead and buried (huge surprise!), General Motors, having learned nothing, is in a big push to apply the same brilliant strategy to Chevrolet.

According to The New York Times, General Motors has hired MTV (ohmygod, how cool is that?) to teach them how to sell Chevys to young people.

But unlike Pontiac, which only pissed away media dollars, Chevy is flirting with frittering away its whole culture on people who don't buy cars, don't want cars, and can't afford cars.

According to The Times...

> *"The partnership (with MTV) is intended to transform things as diverse as the milieu at the company's steel-and-glass headquarters, the look of its Chevrolet cars, the dealership structure and the dashboard technology. Even the test drive is being reimagined, since young consumers find riding in a car with a stranger creepy..."*

You wanna talk creepy? Listen to this...

> *"Mr. Martin (the MTV guru-in-charge) has recruited what he calls 'insurgents,' young Chevrolet employees who are willing to change things from the inside and report to him on skeptical executives."*

What a great idea! An internal Gestapo ratting out noncompliant managers. The Cultural Revolution comes to Detroit.

> *"Last summer, (the MTV) team temporarily transformed part of the G.M. lobby into a loftlike space reminiscent of a coffee shop in Austin or Seattle, with graffiti on the walls and skateboards and throw pillows scattered around."*

It just doesn't get any cooler than Seattle or Awestin. But, with all due respect, you can keep your damn coffee. Where's the weed?

This one killed me:

> *"We tried to teach dealers how to calibrate conversations"*

Yeah, that oughtta work. I can just hear the training session now:

> *MTV GURU: You really need to learn how to calibrate conversations...*
> *CAR DEALER: Calibrate this, asshole.*

A lot has changed since I started in advertising. But one thing will never change: Marketers' brainless, pathetic pursuit of young people.

RECOGNIZING FOOLISHNESS IN EVERYONE
BUT OURSELVES

One of the great truisms of marketing is that a good deal of consumer behavior makes no sense.

While we often go out of our way to scour Google for the lowest prices and the best reviews, we also frequently behave in ways that defy common sense. When it comes to buying stuff, or any other human activity for that matter, we are not logic machines.

Back when I worked on Toyota, there was a great example of this. The Toyota Corolla was built at a plant here in California that was a joint venture between Toyota and Chevrolet. In addition to the Corolla, the plant also built the Chevy Geo Prism, which was the exact same car as the Corolla.

The Prism was built on the same line, by the same people, in the same plant as the Corolla. The only difference was that at the end of the line someone would either put a Corolla badge or a Prism badge on the car. The Corolla cost $1,500 more than the Prism, yet it outsold it 3 to 1.

We in the ad business are always reminding our clients that consumer behavior is not always rational. We lecture them on the importance of emotion as a factor in buying decisions and brand preferences. We explain to them that an ad is not a court case in which the best argument wins.

And yet, while we are exquisitely sensitive to the illogical nature of consumer behavior, we are completely oblivious to illogical behavior in our own business decisions. Our business decisions are just as illogical and just as governed by emotions as consumer buying decisions.

An example:

Last week I spent a few days in San Diego attending conferences that, in part, were about marketing to people over 50.

To give you an example of how astoundingly illogical the actions of the marketing and advertising industries are, I think this one fact should do it:

If people over 50 in the U.S. were a country, they would be the third largest economy in the world:

1. USA

2. China

3. Americans over 50

They are bigger economically than Japan, Germany, or Martin Sorrell.

We in advertising and marketing have all kinds of fairy stories and stupid bullshit excuses for why we don't advertise to these people. The truth is we don't advertise to them for reasons that are completely illogical and fully emotional.

- We don't like being associated with old people
- We like to feel young and hip
- We can't build a successful career on marketing to older people

Consequently, we have invented all kinds of reasons why we ignore them.

One of the great failures of the advertising industry is how clueless we are to our own prejudices and illogical behaviors. We know how to recognize foolishness in everyone but ourselves.

TOP 10 MISTAKES WHEN ADVERTISING TO GROWN-UPS

One of these days your phone is going to ring. Your boss is going to want to see you in his office. He will say, "What is the biggest opportunity for growth we are currently missing?"

You are going to mumble and fumble.

He'll say, "It's people over 50 you dimwit. They account for almost 50% of all consumer spending. They control over 70% of the financial assets of the country. They account for 55% of all CPG purchases. They buy over 60% of all new cars. And we are not spending a goddamn dime talking to them."

Then you will give him all the pathetic excuses that marketing people always come up with and he will fire your ass and have you escorted out of the building with all your crap in a cardboard box, and you will never work again.

Don't let this happen to you!

Marketers who are awake and responsive are starting to understand that there is enormous upside in talking to people over 50. But there are also pitfalls.

The best thing you can do is hire Type A to help you develop a sensible 50+ initiative for your brand. The next best thing you can do is avoid these 10 mistakes:

1. Do not hold up a mirror. Don't try to show them who they are or tell them what they believe. They don't appreciate being treated like advertising clichés.

2. They are not grandma and grandpa. They are Barack Obama and Jerry Seinfeld and Meryl Streep and Condoleezza Rice and Bruce Springsteen. Your copywriters have no clue how to talk to them.

3. Don't be afraid to be naughty. These people grew up smoking weed and listening to the Rolling Stones. Don't be so serious. Make fun of young people. Make them feel hipper than young people. And speaking of young people...

4. They do not want to be like young people. Don't listen to the jokers who tell you "old people aspire to be like young people." This nonsense is 30 years out of date. Older people want to be youthful, but they do not want to be like young people.

5. They are not down-sizing. In 2010 people over 45 outspent people under 45 by one *trillion* dollars.

6. They are not "stuck in their ways" and unchangeable. According to Nielsen, they are just as likely to change brands as people under 50.

7. They are not just the spill from your 18-49 media plan. You need to speak to them directly and differently. This is not simply about media choices. It's also about message.

8. They are not a collection of maladies. Don't talk to them like they're a bundle of afflictions needing remediation. They are not. They are mostly healthy, wealthy and wise. They want to have fun, not medicine.

9. Avoid casting clichés. Please, no more grandpa and Timmy going fishing. No more silver foxes sitting in bath tubs. No more goofy grandmas.

10. "They don't matter in my category." Bullshit. They matter in every category. Whether you're selling dog food or donuts, they matter. They spend almost half the money in this country. Hello?

Now get your 50+ strategy going before that phone call comes.

Chapter Six:

Socially Awkward

THE SLOW PAINFUL COLLAPSE OF
THE SOCIAL MEDIA FANTASY

Part 1

It was going to change business forever. It was going to make traditional advertising irrelevant. It was going to revolutionize marketing.

It was social media marketing. And it's been the biggest disappointment since the NFL hired referees.

While advocates for social media still cling to the wreckage of "the conversation" and continue to hound us with apocryphal tales of social media magic, dispassionate observers are starting to realize what a delusion the whole theory of social media marketing has been.

The idea that consumers were enthusiastic about having conversations about brands online, and they would activate their network of friends and followers to share their enthusiasms and create a socially transmitted tsunami of sales has proven to be deeply fanciful.

It turns out that the average consumer has a lot more on her mind than conducting online conversations about fabric softener.

While people with a financial or ideological stake in social media continue to propagate the fantasy, those annoying, troublesome things called facts keep popping up to undermine their careless assertions.

The first crack in the wall came in 2011 when the largest, boldest experiment in social media marketing ever attempted — the Pepsi Refresh Project — was exposed as a nasty failure that seems to have cost the brand 5% of its market share, which it has never recovered.

Then in September of 2012, Forrester Research reported that...

> *"Social tactics are not meaningful sales drivers. While the hype around social networks as a driver of influence in eCommerce continues to capture the attention of online executives, the truth is that social continues to struggle and registers as a barely negligible source of sales..."*

A few months later, a story in The Wall Street Journal reported on a study IBM had done on the effect of social media on Black Friday sales. While sales were great, the social media contribution to sales were essentially nonexistent.

IBM reported that shoppers referred from Social Networks such as Facebook, Twitter, LinkedIn and YouTube generated less than half of 1% of all online sales on Black Friday. The Journal commented... *"...there's one notable under-performer in the online shopping frenzy: social media."*

But perhaps the most damning report on the negligible influence that social media marketing has on sales was issued a few days ago by McKinsey and Company.

This sentence from the report says it all: *"Email remains a more effective way to acquire customers than social media - nearly 40 times that of Facebook and Twitter combined."*

The social media fantasy is in a death spiral. Social media marketing is no longer taken seriously as a sales builder by anyone with a functioning cortex.

Social media marketing will continue to be popular and sporadically effective in some categories. But when it comes to serious brands, in the vast majority of cases it is evolving into just another cost of doing business.

Part 2

It seems like only yesterday we couldn't turn on the TV, open a magazine, or go to a website without someone exhorting us to "join the conversation."

"The conversation" was the physical proof of the marketing industry's love affair with social media. The idea was that people were highly interested in our brands and would be eager to chat and share their enthusiasms on line with other people.

The philosophical seeds of this conviction were planted in the mid-1990's when it was postulated that the "interruption model" of advertising had run its course. The theory went something like this:

consumers were no longer responsive to advertising messages like TV spots, radio spots, and magazine ads which interrupted their activities. Instead, marketing was transitioning into a period in which the "permission model" would dominate.

The "permission model" posited that in order to be effective, marketers had to stop "interrupting" people with advertising, and instead gain their permission to market to them.

The way you got permission was to engage consumers with useful, interesting messages (often described as "content") that gave consumers value instead of sales pitches. If you did this, they would trust you, like you more, and permit you to market directly to them. In marketing terminology, they would "opt in" to your marketing programs.

Best of all, they would share their passion for your brand with their network of friends and followers who would, likewise, share with their network. A multiplier effect would be born.

There was only one problem with this wonderful proposition. It misinterpreted consumer behavior by substantially overestimating consumers' fervor for brands, and concomitantly misjudging consumers' inclination to share their presumed fervor.

Believers in this ideology assumed that a person's use of a product was a demonstration of enthusiasm for the brand. Sadly, in the vast majority of cases, it is merely an indication of habit, convenience, or mild satisfaction. It is not proof of devotion or enthusiasm.

Regardless of the time, energy and money we spend "differentiating" our brands, most people see very little difference between our brand and our closest competitor's. While there are some brands that people do have great loyalty to, and some categories that people are truly interested in, these are the rare exceptions. In most cases people will change brands with very little bother if it turns out to be convenient or otherwise beneficial.

Most people will gladly switch from Skippy to Jif if they can save a buck or two. If the ballpark doesn't serve Coke, most people will happily return to their seats with a Pepsi.

The idea that social media would become a channel in which consumers would share their strong enthusiasms by having "conversations about brands" has turned out to be a delusion.

Most brands are finding that their social media programs are more time-consuming, more expensive, and less capable of driving sales growth than was promised. Consequently, they are abandoning the "permission model" and reverting to the "interruption model" in their online advertising.

You can see this most clearly on Facebook. Facebook calls itself a social medium, but its business model is good old-fashioned paid advertising plastered all over the page. Compare the number of paid ads you see on your Facebook page with the number of "conversations about brands."

The reason is clear: marketers are finding that they can get more value out of the web by treating it as a venue for advertising, not conversations.

Social media sites are quickly evolving into just another channel for delivering traditional interruptive advertising.

Social media is not going to die or go away. It will continue to grow. But the fantasy of consumers having conversations about brands and sharing their passion for brands — and the claim that this will replace or surpass traditional paid advertising — is simply collapsing as the evidence rolls in.

The "conversation" was a nice idea. It would be lovely if consumers were as eager to share their enthusiasm for our brands as we are. Sadly, they have other things on their minds.

It turns out that "the conversation" has been mostly a monologue.

WHY ARE AGENCY BLOGS SO UNPOPULAR

Agencies are often asked this question: If advertising is so effective, why don't you do it?

The answer they usually give is this: Our potential customer group (target audience) is so small that mass market advertising is imprudent. Instead we use marketing techniques that are more productive for a company like ours that needs to talk to a very small group of prospects one at a time.

This semi-baloney usually satisfies the questioner.

But this excuse only holds up because buying traditional advertising is expensive. The same excuse can't be invoked for social media or content marketing. That stuff is free.

Agencies are constantly haranguing their clients about the need to harness the magic of social media and content marketing — and the expertise they can deliver if the client will just pay them to do it — and yet the social media and content marketing efforts of agencies is somewhere between pathetic and non-existent.

Blogs are a perfect example. I recently checked two websites that measure the popularity of advertising and marketing blogs. Put both lists of top 50 advertising and marketing blogs together and you find exactly one agency blog among them. One.

Now if I'm not mistaken, agencies are supposed to be the experts at social media and content. I mean, companies pay them handsomely to produce this stuff.

Considering that virtually every agency in the universe has some kind of blog, and considering their "unique expertise" at producing "compelling content" and their amazing online marketing skills, you'd think agencies would dominate the lists of advertising and marketing blogs.

Why don't they?

There are only two possible explanations. The first is that they are not capable of creating anything that anyone wants to read. I doubt that this is the reason.

I think the real reason is the second possibility — they're full of shit.

They tell their clients to invest in the awesome power of social media and content marketing, but they are unwilling to do it themselves. They won't spend their own time and money on this magic, but they're eager to spend their clients'.

Apparently what's good for the goose is not good for the gander. After all, the goose lays golden eggs

.

FACEBOOK'S ABOUT FACE

Here at the Ketel One Conference Center of The Ad Contrarian Global Headquarters, we've been talking lately about the remarkable success that Facebook has achieved.

Not only have we been talking about it, we've been high-fiving ourselves and taking full credit for it.

Perhaps you remember Facebook in its initial incarnation. It was the social media upstart that was going to slay the traditional advertising dragon. Well, it seems that it has done just the opposite. It has become a juggernaut of traditional paid advertising.

Some of the baloney that Facebook first tried to sell us was:

-Consumers wanted to "join the conversation" about brands on line.

-Social media marketing was going to make traditional advertising obsolete.

But according to The New York Times...

"Facebook has changed its pitch and the products it offers advertisers so often that many marketing executives are wary."

Now, Facebook is making money hand over fist, its stock value has soared, and they've done it by completely abandoning their initial principles and implementing the semi-brilliant marketing advice of a certain Luddite dinosaur blogger.

A couple of years ago a piece appeared in this space entitled *Either Facebook Is Nuts Or I Am*. The piece made a few points:

First, was that Facebook's "precision targeting" strategy was dumb.

"Why would a company that can reach a billion people...want to sell targeting? They should be selling anti-targeting. They should be selling reach. They are the only media property in the solar system that reaches a billion people (yet) they are trading on their ability to find left-handed falafel lovers in Yonkers. They're sitting on a gold mine, but they're throwing away the gold and selling

the dirt."

Second was that they had to abandon the social media marketing fantasy and realize they were in the advertising sales business...

"...the Z-man has to get used to the idea that he's in the ad business... he has to get rid of all the Global Chief Engagement Content Relationship Jargonators. He has to get some ad sales people who know what the f/k they're selling, and then give them something worthwhile to sell. "

Third, they needed to forget about the little postage stamp ads they were peddling and develop some ad units that had impact.

"They need to offer big-time advertisers something of real value, not the crap they are currently selling."

Two recent reports, one in The New York Times and one in The Wall Street Journal, indicate that Facebook management have become assiduous readers of a certain nutty old ad guy. First, they are soft-pedaling the precision targeting and emphasizing the mass reach. Reporting on a meeting that Facebook's sales staff had with a big client, The Times reporter says...

"At the meeting (Facebook's) ad strategists were saying they wanted (the client) to spend money to show ads to every American woman 45 and older on Facebook — as many as 32 million people."

Next, they have pretty much abandoned the social media baloney...

"A few years ago, the company was telling brands to increase the number of people following their pages. Now it says fans are largely irrelevant."

And finally, they have gotten rid of the no-impact crappy little side bar ads and replaced them with big fat ads right in the middle of your feed. The Journal also describes...

"..a changed format for Facebook's right-hand column ads. They're now larger..."

Unfortunately, old habits die hard. Even though Facebook is no longer kidding themselves about what business they're in, the slow learners in agencies and marketing departments still don't get it. According to a piece in MediaPost, Facebook just signed a $100,000,000 advertising deal with marketing giant RB. Here's what a clueless RB jargonmeister had to say:

"This is not about advertising, but rather about collaboration to drive growth for RB brands and engagement on Facebook,"

Thank goodness. For a minute there I thought this might be about advertising.

7 FABULOUS WAYS TO MAKE LINKEDIN LESS BORING

Let's face it. LinkedIn is a freaking snore.

Unless you're a demented stalker or desperately looking for a job, what the hell is LinkedIn good for? I've been on it for about five years now and I still have no idea why.

The only thing it has to offer is a constant stream of tediously earnest essays called *"The Future Of Data Driven Infometrics."*

Let's be honest here…none of us really gives a shit about the future of anything except ourselves. The only data you really want from LinkedIn is something that can make you some money, take you out of the hell hole you're working in, get you laid, or at least provide you with some amusement at the misfortune of people you can't stand. Am I right?

So I have some ideas for the folks over at LinkedIn. Create a few categories of stuff that you actually care about.

Here are some suggestions for totally compelling information about the people you are connected to that LinkedIn could provide and would make it way more interesting:

1. *People who were born on the same day as you but look way older.*

2. *People you used to work with who hate you and are checking to see if you're dead.*

3. *Super-hot nymphos who anonymously checked your profile.*

4. *CEOs you know who have criminal records.*

5. *Awful guys you once slept with when you were drunk and never called you and are now unemployed.*

6. *People who have fabulously nasty stories about your boss.*

7. *People you are connected to who have extra Super Bowl tickets.*

See what I mean? If LinkedIn had shit like this, I'd like them on Facebook.

BRAND LOYALTY AND SOCIAL MEDIA

Of all the factors relating to consumer behavior, perhaps none is more misinterpreted and mischaracterized than brand loyalty.

While we all have favorite brands in several categories, in most cases our loyalty is an inch deep.

In the agency world, where the religion of branding is unquestioned and inviolable, the misunderstanding of brand loyalty is epidemic.

It is true that, all things being equal, people will default to their favorite brand. But every intelligent marketer knows that her competitors are up late every night working to make sure that all things are *never* equal.

Which brings us to one of the dumbest social media campaigns I have ever read about. And believe me, that's a very high bar.

Apparently an agency in Norway decided that Facebook "engagement" is more import than actual customers. And so they embarked on an astoundingly misguided promotion to trade "likes" for customers. And lost.

The agency somehow convinced Burger King to give free coupons for a Big Mac to anyone who followed Burger King on Facebook on the condition that if they took the coupon they couldn't access a new Facebook page Burger King was launching. In other words, you had to turn down the offer of a free Big Mac to access the new BK page.

According to Ad Age, 38,000 people took part in this campaign. Of the people who did, only 8,000 chose to stick with BK. 30,000 opted for the free Big Mac coupon. But in a very nasty little trick, Burger King only had 1,000 Big Mac coupons to give out to 30,000 people.

The agency is trumpeting the fact that 8,000 people would not accept the coupon and chose to follow Burger King's new Facebook page. Big fucking deal.

So BK now has 8,000 "more engaged" customers (whatever the hell that means) and 29,000 formerly happy customers who are pissed-off because they wanted a Big Mac and BK cheaped-out on them.

Perhaps worst of all, this dumb-ass idea demonstrated to the world how little true loyalty BK's followers had — 79% of their Facebook "fans" opted for the Big Mac.

The ridiculous religion of social media has reached such a point of absurdity that this is being hailed as another great marketing achievement.

I'm sure the visionaries behind this nonsense will be speaking and doing victory laps at the next worldwide social media conference.

HOW THE HIGGS BOSON CAN HELP YOU
BUILD CUSTOMER ENGAGEMENT

Yes, the recent discovery of the Higgs Boson by scientists at the Large Hadron Collider at CERN changes everything for marketers.

First, it poses a huge challenge. How will you use the Higgs Boson to build stronger engagement between your brand and your customers?

Scientists tell us that without the Higgs Boson, matter would have no mass. There would be no stars, no galaxies, and no cinnamon raisin bread. Without mass, we would have no mass media and no mass transit. Massachusetts would be Achusetts.

The calcified old-world thinking of Madison Avenue, with its TV commercials and display ads, relied on dreary, clunky electrons to deliver a one-way message to a passive viewer. But now, electrons are dead! Today, the particle-wave-connected consumer or, as we like to call him, the average schmuck, is just another bump in an ever-expanding Higgs Field.

Messages embedded in a Higgs Boson bounce right off the average schmuck and create an immediate channel connecting him to someone else — in many cases, a below-average schmuck.

Here's an example of how Higgs Boson marketing works in a worldwide, inter-globulated ecosystem of engagement: Let's say a Higgs Boson passes through my arm. In the next instant it may pass through your foot. Or it might pass through some super-hot nympho's tiny skirt and go bouncing around in her thong. How awesome would that be? (We'd finally get some data-driven insights we could really use. If you get my drift.)

Today, the consumer is dead! Or, she's in total control. I forget. Scientists now estimate that somewhere between 14 and 600 million billion trillion Higgs Bosons penetrate a typical consumer's body every moment. Can you imagine how many would penetrate it if she was totally naked?

According to one theory proposed by physicists at the Very, Very Small Teflon Collider in Rhode Island, there are actually more bosons in the universe than social media consultants in Brooklyn.

Three Ways To Incorporate The Higgs Boson Into Your Marketing Plan Right Now!

1. Remember, activating Higgs Boson technology is only one part of your 360 degree marketing ecosystem. It's actually about 154 degrees. So you still have 206 degrees to play with. Don't neglect all your other important marketing activities like tweeting, podcasting, crank calling, and going to Cannes to snort coke with Swedish account planners.

2. Collecting "likes" on Facebook is still a great way to stay busy without actually accomplishing anything. But it's not too early to start accumulating "Bosos." A "Boso" is like a "like." It occurs when a Boson interacts with another particle and then something amazing happens and your score goes up and you can win a new dining room set.

3. Three words: Gamify your bosons!

WHY I HATE "CONTENT"

In the material world there is no single word that encompasses both art and a beer spill.

There is no word that creates a unity between a Rodin sculpture and a photo of a foot.

There is no term that forges an equivalency between a Gershwin melody and a bloody handkerchief.

In the online world there is such a word. It is "content."

Content is anything you can upload to the web. In other words, it is pretty much anything.

It is a Shakespeare sonnet and a picture of my cat's ass.

It bestows value on anything, and in so doing, debases everything.

It takes the symbol of a witless age - the selfie - and gives it status. You're not guilty of narcisstic self-indulgence, you're creating content!

Worst, it is spoken of with respect. It is, in some quarters, regarded as a serious and compelling expression of online value.

If there has ever been an asset with a lower value, I'd like to know what it is.

We have conferences about content. We have books about content. We have seminars about it, and companies that specialize in it.

Content is everything, and it's nothing. It's an artificial word thrown around by people who know nothing, describing nothing.

It is an excuse masquerading as a resource.

Content is a con.

It is the ultimate Seinfeld episode: it's a show about nothing.

JANET WARREN LIKES WALMART

Janet Warren was one of those impossibly wonderful girls.

Not just pretty, not just smart, but nice and pleasant and friendly. She was a cheerleader with actual cheer. Naturally, she had no idea I existed. But she lived in the next building, and her sister was friendly with my sister.

I was in Los Angeles once, years after high school, and I saw her in a popular restaurant. She was with a group of obviously high-performance individuals, and she was the star of the crowd. I studied her from across the room. She was in her early 30's and had an ethereal almost-hippie, almost-executive look and manner. I found out, years later, that she had been the producer of some pretty important movies.

Years passed and as circumstances sometimes unfold, I had occasion to have lunch with her. I explained to her who I was, and of course, she didn't remember me. She was still lovely in that way that women over 50 can be lovely if they dress simply and tastefully and don't have surgery and don't try to be 20.

She had adopted a child. She was active in many organizations that worked for social justice. She was no longer an active producer, but still had great poise and presence.

We exchanged a few emails following our lunch. I wanted to become friends, but after a while she gracefully stopped emailing, saying she was too busy. I knew what that meant. Several months later I was surprised when she friended me on Facebook.

Lately, on my Facebook page, I find ads that tell me that "Janet Warren Likes Walmart."

If there is one thing that I am certain of in this life it is this — Janet Warren *does not like fucking Walmart*. In fact, I would bet she has never set foot in Walmart. I'd bet that if she knew Walmart was using her to sell their wares, she'd have a stroke.

But that's what Facebook does. It uses you, without your specific permission, to create advertising for its clients. You are the leverage.

It's not like a testimonial in any other medium where they need a signed release to use your name and likeness. Facebook has rigged the system so that if you agree to their terms of service, as far as they're concerned, you are fair game. And if their algorithm likes you, then you are now the new spokesperson for Walmart. Congratulations.

This is not healthy. It is uber-false advertising. It is not ethical. Our billionaire friends in the tech industry try to pass themselves off as high-minded visionaries. In fact they are turning out to be corrupt and unconcerned about our rights and privacy.

Janet Warren does not like Walmart. But Faceberg is building an unscrupulous empire by claiming she does.

CHEESEGATE: THE AMAZING SAGA OF
THE 45-DAY CHEESE TWEET

If you're looking for a reason to throw yourself under a bus, I suggest reading *"We Got A Look Inside The 45-Day Planning Process That Goes Into Creating A Single Corporate Tweet"* at Business Insider.

It is written by someone who is supposed to be an advertising reporter. But it's written with the clueless insouciance of a wide-eyed sorority girl wandering into a 9-man circle jerk.

The story goes something like this: a bunch of poor bastards are squandering their young lives in a social media "war room" creating useless social media nonsense while the agency bleeds its client for thousands of dollars.

Oops, sorry, I mean a group of social media professionals got an agency in trouble by milking the cow a little too hard.

Cutting to the chase here, the article tells the story of "13 social-media and advertising specialists" who took 45 days to "plan, create, approve, and publish" a tweet about cheese.

One fucking tweet — 45 days!

Why? Because only social media specialists can be that fucking stupid.

It takes me 30 *seconds* to write a tweet and that's because I type with my feet. The New York Times can publish a 50-page newspaper every day of the year, but these cement-heads need 45 days to create a tweet.

Can you imagine how much money the agency made on that tweet?

You have to read the details of this folly to appreciate the lunacy of it. According to the reporter, someone from the agency's social media team...

> *"...met with a copywriter and graphic designer to brainstorm tweet ideas for the next month. It was then that the copywriter suggested a tweet centered on the idea that Camembert, a French cheese popular during the spring, was best served at room temperature. The copywriter and designer met the next week to create the image for the tweet, which*

> *was then pitched at a team meeting...The meeting includes (the social*
> *media genius), the copywriter, a designer team, and a project manager.*
> *Then it's on to an internal review, where senior copywriters and*
> *strategists sign off on the work over the course of the following week.*
> *The post was then sent to Président Cheese and, some 45 days after*
> *conception, published on the internet for the world to see."*

The world to see? This company has 100 followers on Twitter. My hernia scar has more followers.

And what was the result of this monumental whack-a-thon? This shining star of brilliance:

Can you imagine what this masterpiece would have been like if they only had 44 days?

Here's the best part. The tweet was posted on April 30th. As of May 24th it had zero retweets and two "favorites" (I'm guessing *Le Président* and his *mama*.)

I can tweet a picture of my cat's ass and get fifty times better results. On the other hand, my cat's ass looks a lot better than this incomprehensible photo.

Remarkably, the writer for Business Insider seemed to think this astounding absurdity was admirable and praiseworthy instead of being one of the most insanely wasteful and idiotic abuses of "marketing" the world has ever seen.

As soon as the social media crowd got hold of this story, the cheese really hit the fan. And the Donald Sterling Effect reared its ugly head. You see, people who screw up have a compulsion to make things worse by trying to justify their screw-up. So here comes the agency's planning director to the rescue. He wrote a piece for a trade magazine defending the agency.

In the piece he did a little switcheroo and played it like the article claimed it had taken 45 days to write the tweet...

"Of course it doesn't take 45 days to write a Tweet."

The piece said no such thing. It made it very clear that the 45 days included creative development, planning, meetings, internal reviews, and whatever other useless bullshit the agency could bill the client for.

He then went on to defend their planning process...

"As social has grown from a discipline emerging from the sidelines into a core pillar of the wider digital landscape, it also benefits from the increased professionalism behind the approach."

Really? When the fruits of your "discipline emerging from the sidelines" get zero retweets and two favorites, maybe it's better to save the baloney about "increased professionalism" for another day.

Look, I'm hoping this story never ends because it's rare to find a story that's both a laugh riot and a click magnet. But, honestly, you don't spend time in the agency business without eventually screwing something up royally. We've all done it. Everyone understands it.

So because I love all my children, here's some free advice for the agency — quit the whining and take your medicine.

Issue the following statement: "Sometimes process can be the enemy of progress. We've learned something from this and are streamlining everything we do."

Then do yourself a favor. Shut the fuck up.

WHY YOUR SOCIAL MEDIA STRATEGY SUCKS

You've probably noticed that about 93% of all TV commercials are lousy. And so are about the same percent of movies, TV shows, books, songs, and paintings.

If you think all this crappy stuff is around because people aren't trying very hard, you're wrong. The reason is actually quite simple: Producing good stuff is really, really hard. And there are very few people who can do it.

Nobody sets out to create a crappy TV spot or a crappy book or a crappy song. They just turn out that way.

Creative talent is a very rare and very precious commodity. Not everyone has it. As a matter of fact, hardly anyone has it.

That's why really good creative people — whether singers, writers, actors, and even us ad bozos — often make a lot of money.

Fortunately, most of us don't think of ourselves as singers, writers, painters and actors. So the quantity of really shitty "art" is self-limiting. This is not the case, however, in social media.

Everyone thinks he's a capable social media creator. Believe it or not, there are actually more English language blogs in the world than there are English language native speakers.

If you're wondering why your blog, or your Facebook page, or your Twitter feed, or your "compelling" content, or your "viral" video is laying around doing nothing, it's not hard to figure. In order to be interesting, social media requires creativity — just like movies, TV shows, music, and writing.

Without creativity, nobody gives a shit. The world is full of dull opinions, almost-funny banter, and dreary monographs.

Your social media strategy doesn't suck because Facebook, Twitter, YouTube and blogs can't reach people. It sucks because you're stuffing it with crap that no one is interested in.

Creativity is the ability to be interesting, funny, or different. It's easy to be interesting, funny or different at lunch.

It's a thousand times more difficult to do it on a page.

Chapter Seven:

Fraud, Corruption And Other Fun Web Activities

WHAT EVERY CEO NEEDS TO KNOW ABOUT
ONLINE ADVERTISING

Dear Mr. CEO,

I am writing to you as a friend.

I was once a ceo myself. In fact, I was ceo of two different advertising agencies.

Consequently, I understand how difficult it is for you to know everything that is going on in your organization. But there is something you need to know. If your company is spending money on online advertising, you are almost certainly being robbed.

Here are some facts:

Google reported last week that 56% of online display ads that are paid for by advertisers are never seen by a live human being. (And remember, Google is one of the world's largest sellers of online display ads.)

Recently The New York Times ran a story claiming that 57% of online video ads are never seen.

CNET reported on a study by research firm Incapsula that found only 38% of traffic on the web is human.

Kraft announced that it was rejecting 75-85% of the online ad impressions it was being offered because they were "fraudulent, unsafe, non-viewable or unknown."

Adweek, one of the advertising industry's leading trade publications, estimated that online ad fraud in the U.S. may have reached $9.5 billion last year.

I am sure that your marketing people will tell you that they have systems or people in place that protect you from this corruption. They don't. No one knows the extent of the fraud. No one even knows how to determine the extent of the fraud. Online ad fraud is completely out of control.

A company in the advertising fraud detection business recently estimated that just one average sized bot-net could be responsible for one billion fraudulent ad impressions every day.

There are 3 types of fraud you are exposed to:

    1. Intentional fraud: Here's how The Economist describes it: "Evil-doers infect personal computers with a "bot", a piece of software that visits websites in the background. It cannot be detected by the user, and is nearly impossible for advertisers to spot, because it shares the real user's unique "cookie" identifier. Fraudsters have other tricks too: they can stack hundreds of adverts on top of each other on a website, or stuff a whole website into a small pixel on a page so advertisers think their ads are seen. Either way, they are deliberately claiming "views" and "clicks" for ads that no one ever sees."

    2. Unintentional fraud: The online ad world is so arcane and opaque, people are unknowingly buying and selling ad inventory that exists only in a technical sense — it does not exist in the real word. This is euphemistically called the "viewability" problem. In the article cited above, The New York Times describes how people have no idea where their online advertising is running.

    3. Unknown fraud: Once again, the online ad world is so complex and impenetrable, there may very well be types of fraud we haven't even discovered.

As I'm sure you know, all forms of advertising are subject to waste. This is because not everyone notices every ad. This is just the nature of advertising. Apologists for online advertising try to excuse the fraud as just another example of ad waste. It is not.

The waste in online ads is of another magnitude. First, criminals are stealing your money. Then, unviewable ad placements are siphoning more of your money. And after all that, what's left is still subject to the normal waste of advertising.

Your marketing people will not tell you about this corruption and fraud because they do not want to look like fools. Your agency will not tell you about it because they are afraid they will be blamed.

If you are a substantial online advertiser, you are almost certainly a victim of this fraud.

I spent over forty years in the advertising business, and in that time I never saw anything like the corruption and double-dealing that is currently being perpetrated by the online advertising industry. I have no skin in this game. I don't own a TV station or a magazine or billboards. I'm just a retired ad guy who doesn't like to see my industry corrupted.

You are being screwed. I thought you'd like to know.

Love always,

Bob

SNEAKY LITTLE BASTARDS

For years, the Truth and Reconciliation Commission here at Ad Contrarian World Headquarters has been determined to expose the unreliable nature of most of what you read about digital advertising. There are three reasons for this:

1. The digital industry is full of sneaky little bastards whose "facts" and "data" usually turn out to be either intentionally misleading, willfully incomplete, or stone cold bullshit.

2. The research industry, heavily dependent on the digital ad industry for business, is complicit and almost always spins its findings about digital in the most positive light.

3. The pitiful trade press — devoid of perspective or skepticism — swallows this garbage whole and publishes it with a tone of gee-whiz boosterism that would embarrass a high school newspaper editor.

Which brings me to last week. My life is so empty and pathetic that I was actually reading Ad Age one night.

I came upon an article concerning the remarkable effectiveness of digital ads in magazine tablet (tablet as in iPad) editions. Here's what I read:

> *"Starch Digital used online surveys to measure consumer recall of more than 13,000 ads in magazine tablet editions during the second half of 2012. We found that nearly 9,500 of those ads offered interactive features — and that half of the people surveyed who read or noted those went ahead and interacted in some way."*

I was amazed. I know that fewer than one person in a thousand interacts with display advertising in general. And yet, here we have a report of half the people interacting.

Soon I turned out the light and went to sleep. Except I couldn't sleep. My experience in advertising told me this report was highly unlikely. My experience as a former science teacher told me it was completely impossible.

I was lying there for at least twenty minutes thinking. And then it struck me. I turned the light back on and re-read the piece. And there it was. To a casual, unsuspecting reader the impression was that half the people interacted with the ads. But what it actually said was that "half of the people surveyed who read or noted those ads went ahead and interacted in some way."

In other words, you had to either read the ad or "note" it (I think that means remember seeing it) to be counted. So if only 1% of people read or noted it, then the true level of interaction was not 50%, but 50% of 1%, or .5%.

Of course, neither Starch nor Ad Age told us what percent of people "read or noted" the ads because that would be way too open and honest. So we have no way to know the true level of interaction.

All we know is that, according to Starch...

> *"...large numbers of consumers...interacted with ads for gas and oil drilling investments, a book about Proust, a store catering solely to runners and walkers, and exercises to improve one's golf game."*

A large number of people interacted with an ad for a book about Proust? That's when I knew this whole thing was bullshit.

So, if "large numbers interacted," Mr. Starch, why don't you give us all the information so we can decide for ourselves whether the numbers are "large" or not?

But here's the thing. Even if they did give us the full picture it would still be meaningless. Their definitions were so absurdly biased in favor of "interaction" that the numbers mean nothing .

For example, some of the ads were video ads that started up *automatically*. By sitting there and doing nothing, you were counted as interacting when the video started.

Some of the ads were very small and were essentially unreadable unless you expanded the ad. And once you expanded it, you were automatically counted as "interacting." For people who expanded the ads to read them, there was no difference between reading the ad and interacting with it. When Ad Age said...

"...half of the people surveyed who read or noted those ads went ahead and interacted in some way..." they had not done their homework, as usual. A great many of the people who expanded the ad to read it didn't "go ahead and interact in some way." But they were counted as interacting.

And get this — of the people who were counted as interacting, the largest group was the group that just clicked or touched the ad to expand it.

Hey, Starch, here's an idea. Why not count clicking the "X" to get rid of the ad as an interaction? That should make your masters happy.

But wait, there's even more.

Being fascinated by this exercise in deceptive nonsense, I went to Starch's PR release about this study to see what they had to say. Here's what I found...

> "More than half of consumers who read a magazine ad on their tablet or e-reader interacted with the ad, according to new research covering more than 30,000 digital ads across 1,000 magazine issues from GfK MRI Starch Digital...The research shows that 55% of digital magazine readers "noted," or read, a digital advertisement on their tablet or e-reader..."

What's your take-away from this? If you are not thinking like a sneaky little bastard, one of your take-aways is probably that people read 55% of the digital magazine ads they were exposed to. But that's not what it means at all.

What the language actually means is that during the 6-month test period, 55% of people *ever* read or noted a digital magazine ad. In other words, if you were exposed to 1,000 digital magazine ads during this 6-month period, it doesn't mean you read 55% (550) of them, it means there's a 55% chance you read *one of them*!

In my hundreds of years in the ad business I have witnessed more bullshit than I care to admit. But I've never experienced a more persistent and unrelenting effort to distort and mislead than I have seen from the digital advertising industry and its unprincipled flunkies.

ALARMING ONLINE SLEAZE FACTOR

If they gave awards for reporting on the advertising industry (and why not, they give awards for everything else) this year's award should go to Mike Shields of Adweek whose work on the corruption and fraud in the online ad industry has been outstanding.

This is by far the biggest advertising story of the year, and no one but Mike and I seem to be interested in it.

His latest piece, *The Amount of Questionable Online Traffic Will Blow Your Mind* ran a few days ago and should be required reading for anyone who buys display advertising.

The article asserts that,

> "...the online ad industry is facing a swelling crisis, one defined by fake traffic, bogus publishers and invisible Web visitors... bogus ad inventory, as it turns out, is rampant. In fact, according to numerous sources across the ecosystem, fake traffic is essentially systemic to advertising—it's part of how the business works."

In a previous article Mike wrote,

> "If you spend enough time in the murky world of ad exchanges, ad tech middlemen and real-time bidding software, you might come away wondering why any major brand even bothers with online advertising. Not only are banners dull and clickthrough rates low, but all the technology flooding the industry promising perfect targeting perfection can't even deliver real human audiences..."

Mike reports that the world of online advertising is so screwed-up, corrupt, and incomprehensible that at times it is impossible to know what you are buying or whom you are buying it from...

> "...According to (independent trading desk) Digilant COO Nate

Woodman, the situation is so ungovernable that the agency has found instances where it's ended up buying impressions from itself."

The problem is that no one wants to kill the golden goose. Naive advertisers are getting stuck with billions in worthless, nonexistent "advertising."

"John Snyder, CEO of the keyword-targeting firm Grapeshot, says he's lost business because his company won't sell bad inventory. "We'll hear, 'Your competitor got great clicks,' but all on two sites and it was all fraud. But it's these optimization algorithms that find those clicks.' "

The fraudulent practices aren't just limited to banner ads...

"While the display market has seen dicey practices growing for a while now, the challenge of bad inventory is suddenly escalating in video..."

Is anything changing? Says Woodman (of Digilant)...

"When we try to tighten things up, our measured performance goes down...We need to fix this as an industry," he adds. "Somebody needs to give a shit."

Last month, we ran a post about this subject that speculated that as much as $9.5 billion in online advertising is either fraudulent or invisible.

Unfortunately, nobody is going to "give a shit" until somebody goes to jail.

ATTACK OF THE BILLIONAIRE HYPOCRITES

The Silicon Valley aristocracy, who have made billions and billions by collecting ungodly amounts of personal information about us, came out in force yesterday to denounce governments for collecting ungodly amounts of personal information about us.

They're shocked — shocked I tell you! — at the intrusion into our privacy.

I have two words for these greedy, lying, hypocrites: screw you.

You are the people who enabled this. You are the people who chose to ignore what was obvious to everyone with a functioning brain — that your relentless collection of information about private citizens is totally at odds with the principles of democracy.

Here's what the despicable hypocrites of Google, Facebook, Twitter, Apple, Yahoo, LinkedIn, Microsoft and AOL had to say yesterday:

"The undersigned companies believe that it is time for the world's governments to address the practices and laws regulating government surveillance of individuals and access to their information."

Here's what I think:

"The undersigned citizen (that's me!) believes that it is time for the world's web scumbags to address their practices and rules regarding web plutocrats surveillance of individuals and access to their information."

Let me tell you something Google, Facebook, Twitter, Apple, Yahoo, LinkedIn, Microsoft and AOL — you puffed-up, self-important, arrogant phonies — you have the smell of this all over you. Pretending that you are suddenly the stalwart guardians of peoples' privacy makes me sick.

If a dumbass blogger could figure out what was going on, don't pretend that you couldn't. Three years ago, almost to the day – long before all this NSA shit hit the fan — the aforementioned dumbass blogger published an article called *Big Brother Has Arrived And He's Us*. In the article he wrote:

> *The essence of freedom and democracy is being undermined. The Internet now knows everything about us. It knows where we go, who we talk to, what we talk about... It knows our locations at any moment and whom we are with... It knows our political beliefs and our sexual hab- its... It knows what our ailments are, what drugs we use, what doctors we see and what our psychological profiles are. It pretends the information is secure, but only a blind fool believes this... And why does it do all this?... for the marketing and advertising industries... There is no realistic vision of the future in which this will not lead to appalling mischief.*
>
> *It's time to put aside our petty self-interest, take a step back and see where this is leading. We need to stop tracking people and their behavior now. Right now.*

I know what your posturing is about. It's about money. You are afraid that people are starting to realize what malignant jackals you are. And you're trying to delegate the blame.

I'd like to know exactly what the difference is between "tracking" and "surveillance?"

Physician... you know the rest.

THE SCAM WHAT AM

For several months, the Investigative Helicopter Team here at The Ad Contrarian Global Headquarters has been writing about the masssive fraud being perpetrated on online advertisers.

This week, Jack Marshall of Digiday has a great interview with a former online scam artist — oops, I mean publishing executive — who tells his story. Here are some of the highlights:

- Why he bought traffic he knew was fraudulent:

"As a website running an arbitrage model, all that mattered was profit, and for every $0.002 visit we were buying, we were making between $0.0025 and $0.004 selling display ads through networks and exchanges."

- How did he know it was bots, not humans, he was buying?

"When we told them we were looking for the cheapest traffic we could possibly buy there would be sort of a wink and a nod, and they'd make us aware that for that price the traffic would be of "unknown quality"... You can tell it's bot traffic just by looking at the analytics."

- Do publishers know they're engaged in fraud?

"Publishers know... Any publisher that's smart enough to understand an arbitrage opportunity is smart enough to understand... What we were doing was 100 percent intentional...I believe publishers are willing to do anything to make their economics work."

- On networks and ad exchanges:

"We worked with a major supply-side platform partner that was just wink wink, nudge nudge about it. They asked us to explain why almost all of our traffic came from one operating system and the majority had all the same user-agent string. There was nothing I could really say.... It was their way of letting us know that...In theory they maintain the quality of their traffic. In reality they just turn a blind eye."

- How widespread is the fraud?

"...there are a lot of people who knowingly do it....There are so many ways they could police this, but the incentive just isn't there."

I've always believed that the ad industry attracted a certain kind of harmless bullshit artist whose assertions were so obviously self-serving and unreliable that no one with an ounce of grey matter would take them seriously.

Apparently I am wrong. We seem to have a large group of online buyers and sellers who are willfully buying and selling fraudulent merchandise. By keeping one step away from the smoking gun, they believe they are able to maintain deniability. Time will tell. Sooner or later, if the foundation is dodgy the house comes tumbling down.

It's a rotten, dirty game and ignorant advertisers are getting skinned alive. The amazing thing is that no one's been arrested or fired.

WHY CLICKS MATTER

I used to be creative director on the Blue Cross account. We did some very nice advertising for Blue Cross. We even won some Clios (no thanks to me, I had great people working for me) back when Clios were worth something.

The primary objective of the advertising was simple — to get people to apply for a Blue Cross policy.

The way we did it was to put 800 numbers in our TV spots and coupons in our print ads. We were clear why we put these response mechanisms into the ads — because they were supposed to elicit a response.

We had an exceedingly stupid client. He insisted on evaluating our performance based on how many policies he sold. On several occasions I tried to explain to him that advertising could not sell his policies.

All advertising could do was get people to either send in the coupon or dial the 800 number. Once they did that, it was out of our hands.

I tried to make it clear to this genius that the only logical way to evaluate our advertising was on how many coupons or phone calls it generated. That was advertising's job. The advertising couldn't answer the phone, talk to the customers, or write an attractive policy. That was his job.

Of course, being an imbecile, he never understood this and if he is still alive and sober somewhere I'm sure he still doesn't.

This is why the people who are trying to convince us that clicks don't matter are so wrong.

Online advertising, in particular banners, were supposed to be interactive. However, when it became clear that interactivity with banners, i.e., clicking, was dangerously close to non-existent, the online ad community began a campaign of propaganda to convince us that clicks don't matter.

They are wrong.

The argument that display ads should be evaluated on sales is wrong. The ad usually can't make a sale, it can only link us to someplace where a sale can be made.

The argument that a display ad should be evaluated as a "branding" mechanism is also unsound. Display ads have very little value as brand builders. They are largely invisible. To my knowledge there is no major brand of any non-web-native product that has ever been built on display advertising.

The only realistic expectation for a display ad is that it will generate a click.

NOBODY EVER CLICKED ON THE MONA LISA

Recently I expressed the opinion that the only sensible expectation for online display advertising is that it will generate a click.

Now that the dirty little secret that almost no one clicks on display ads is out, one of the arguments that apologists, sales hustlers, and people who don't understand advertising drag out is "oh yeah, well nobody ever clicked on a TV spot."

There are several reasons why this argument is appallingly stupid. First is the most obvious. You can't click on a TV spot.

Next, you're not supposed to click on a TV spot.

Next, TV doesn't rely on "interactivity" for effectiveness. TV has an amazing 60-year history of building brands and selling stuff without the supposed magic of interactivity.

Display advertising, on the other hand, was sold to us on the basis of interactivity. Consumers were going to want to engage with it and interact by clicking, which was going to make it so much more effective. Clicking, by the way, is the one and only way to interact with so-called "interactive" advertising. It is why we spend all this money creating hyperlinks and linking things together. Clicks are the connective tissue of the Internet.

What the display crowd are trying to sell us now is the idea that clicks are irrelevant and that display advertising is brilliant for "branding." Only a blind fool believes this nonsense. Every study ever done tells the same story — display ads are overwhelmingly ignored.

The argument that "nobody ever clicked on a TV spot" is the witless, desperate argument of apologists for an over-hyped, marginally effective mode of advertising.

Amazingly, there are people throughout the marketing industry dense enough to accept it.

MISINTERMEDIATION

One of the early principles of online marketing was disintermediation — a typically obnoxious word that digi-dweebs used to mean "eliminating the middle man."

The thinking went like this: Levi's makes jeans. People buy jeans. The web will allow people to buy jeans directly from Levi's and eliminate the unnecessary costs of distribution, promotion, and retailing that are necessitated by middlemen.

Before the tech crash of 2000, it was widely believed that online economic activity would overtake traditional brick-and-mortar activity by allowing disintermediation.

This belief — still held widely by simpletons who have no idea how either humans or businesses work — is still floating around.

As usual, in the delusional world of modern day marketing, the fact that online commerce constitutes just 6% of retail activity and good old brick and mortar retail activity constitutes 94% of retail business activity is of no consequence. Facts don't mean much these days.

To a large extent, the web has not disintermediated anything. Amazon doesn't manufacture clothes, books, bicycles, cameras, CDs, and wine. Neither does eBay. They're just a different kind of middleman that happens to be on line instead of at the mall.

So disintermediation has turned out to be largely a pile of hooey.

Now let's cut to an interesting piece I read this weekend by a guy named John Stoughton. Stoughton's piece is called *"Disintermediation and the Curious Case of Digital Marketing – revisited."*

Stoughton is a communications planner at a UK agency and seems to know his material very well. I say "seems to" because I could only understand about 1/3 of it, but what I understood seemed smart.

Stoughton made several good points, but the one that interested me most was his point that for a medium that was supposed to disintermediate everything it touched, the web has *mis*-intermediated the living hell out of advertising (by the way, misintermediate is my term, don't blame him.)

In fact there is so much misintermediating going on — so many middlemen in the buying, selling, bidding, and placing of online ads — that no one even knows what they are buying or where it is running.

Traditional advertising is pretty simple. I buy the back page of the NY Times news section and I see my ad on the back page of the NY Times news section. When I buy a banner ad, on the other hand, the astonishingly arcane black box of adtech kicks in.

According to a video called *"Behind The Banner"* here's what happens when a web page loads (I have taken the liberty to edit some of their copy):

- When a person visits a web page, a request is initiated for an advertising impression
- An impression request is generated based on what the web page knows about the person
- The impression request is forwarded to the publisher's ad server
- The publisher checks to see if this impression matches any of its pre-sold ad inventory
- If not, it is sent to one of several ad exchanges
- Servers looking to bid on the impression may communicate with other servers to augment the data they have on the person visiting the site
- Next, an auction takes place in which third parties bid on the chance to fulfill the impression
- The impression is sold to the highest bidder, for the second highest bid price
- The banner is then sent to the web page and appears to the user.

This whole thing takes less than 1/4 of a second.

And what is the result of all this complexity and misintermediation? Nobody knows where the hell their ads are running and almost half of online ad impressions have been found to be fraudulent.

Which just goes to prove, once again, that the advertising industry can complicate the shit out of anything.

WILL ADVERTISING CORRUPTION SCANDAL EXPLODE?

Two years ago we wrote, *"Not only are online advertisers getting screwed by crooks, some of them are also getting screwed by their agencies."*

This is suddenly a hot topic.

For over two years, the Crack Investigative Team here at *The Ad Contrarian* Worldwide Headquarters has been reporting on corruption and fraud in advertising — particularly in the online ad industry.

Billions of advertisers' dollars have been stolen, wasted, and misappropriated while everyone who should have been acting responsibly turned a blind eye. There was just too much money at stake.

Meanwhile, pathetically naive and impressionable marketers continue to throw good money after bad.

- *They don't know what they're buying*

- *They don't know whom they're buying it from*

- *They don't know what they're getting*

- *They don't know how much they're paying*

If the victims weren't so fucking dumb, it would be sad. But, honestly, I can't help but be amused.

There are several types of fraud being perpetrated on online advertisers, here are a few of the major ones:

1. *Phony traffic* - Bot-nets generate billions of phony visits to websites daily, which advertisers pay for.

2. *Phony clicks* - Likewise

3. *Phony websites* - Sometimes called "spoofing," phony websites pretend they're real websites and sell imaginary ad space to knuckleheads

4. *Invisible ads* - Euphemistically called "unviewable," these are ads that "technically" appear but are invisible.

5. *Agency kickbacks* - Suddenly, the most topical corruption issue.

The wonderful thing about all these scams is that everybody

thinks it's *the other guy* who's the idiot. They assure their clients and their management that it's the *other guy* being screwed and "we have processes in place to protect ourselves."

Yeah, right.

Meanwhile the crooks and sleazebags are laughing all the way to the bank.

In the past ten days, the trade press has finally come out of its inexplicable torpor and has started to report on the some of the issues, particularly the agency kickback issue.

On March 5, Jon Mandel, former CEO of Mediacom (owned by WPP) told an audience at the Association of National Advertisers Media Leadership Conference about widespread U.S. agency kickbacks.

He presented a document which purported to show how some of the kickbacks work...

> *"...a media agency agreeing with an unnamed media vendor to an industry-standard 2% commission, but as much as 9% in volume-based incentives." (Ad Age)*

Since then, reports of kickbacks have appeared in *The Wall Street Journal*, and several other venues including a front page story in *Ad Age*, that reported...

> *" 'It's really ugly and crooked,' said one ad-tech executive who described receiving such requests."*

> *" 'It's the reason I left,' said a former U.S. media-agency executive."*

Ad Age reports,

> *"U.S.-based marketers are being kept out of the loop about billions of dollars that agencies make back from deals on clients' behalf, according to industry executives, whether in the*

form of opaque markups, kickbacks or undisclosed rebates."

Mandel said,

"Have you ever wondered why fees to agencies have gone down and yet the declared profits to these agencies are up?"

According to The Wall Street Journal...

"Marketers say they're increasingly worried agencies are allocating ad dollars in ways that best suit their own businesses, as opposed to those of their clients."

Brian Wieser, Senior Research Analyst at Pivotal Research Group says...

"...most of the activity involving undisclosed activities is likely concentrated in digital."

But kickbacks are only the tip of the iceberg of fraud and corruption in the digital ad business.

Perhaps the most astounding part of this incipient scandal is that the victims seem determined to hush it up.

While Ad Age reports that "hundreds of millions" of dollars are being siphoned from advertisers, a few days after Mandel's talk, the Association of National Advertisers issued this pathetic statement,

"...we regret any impression that agencies in general are engaged in questionable activities and apologize to those who were offended."

Gag me with a volume-based incentive. Mandel never claimed these practices were universal.

Apparently the victims are afraid that a thorough investigation will expose them for the clueless buffoons they are. After all, if their corporations lose a few hundred million here and there, big deal. Just as long as they don't lose their jobs.

The big question is whether this will erupt into a full-fledged scandal or just fade away behind a curtain of double-talk and indecipherable accounting? The answer lies in discovering whose interest would be served by exposing the corruption of the current system:

-The agencies? Hell no.

-The online media industry? Hell no.

-The marketing doofuses who have been asleep at the wheel? Hell no.

None of the principals have much of an incentive to make trouble. The only hope lies with the press.

If the mainstream press gets on it, and governmental agencies take notice, something useful might happen. Otherwise, corruption as usual.

By the end of this decade online advertising will be as big as TV advertising. The advertising and marketing industries are too deeply invested to make much of a fuss about its unsavory, criminal underbelly.

Will the advertising corruption scandal explode? Count me as officially skeptical.

Chapter Eight:

Contrarianism - Not Just A Job, A Lifestyle

AD EXEC SAYS HE DIDN'T KNOW ANYTHING

CHICAGO — Advertising executive Fenton Schmetz admitted today that all during his successful 18-year advertising career he didn't know anything.

Schmetz, who most recently held the position of Chief Irritation Officer at Compucom, a worldwide, international, global, intercontinental agency said in an interview, "I really don't know anything about advertising or marketing or people or business. I just made things up. I don't even know how to pay my cable bill."

When asked how he was able to fool people for 18 years, Schmetz said, "I would ask people to come into my office and show me what they were working on. Then I would say 'I don't like that' and I would make them change it. After they changed it a few times I would say 'OK, that's better.' Also, sometimes I went to meetings and ate blueberry bagels and nodded my head."

Schmetz said he was first attracted to advertising by the clothing. "I always looked very good in black t-shirts and I thought that if I could just find a job where I could wear a black t-shirt every day I would do very well. Oh, and expensive eye-wear. I always wanted to wear expensive eye-wear. The other thing that attracted me to advertising is that I like friendly girls and I found that advertising has a lot of them."

Schmetz said the most difficult challenge for him during his tenure at Compucom came at lunch. "During the work day it was easy to fool people. I just took the things that everyone else said and moved a few words around. Like, they would say, 'We need a multi-channel solution that leverages our disruption across the ecosystem' and then I'd wait a few minutes and I would say, 'I think we need disruption across the ecosystem that leverages our multi-channel solutions.' Everyone seemed to agree."

"That part was easy. The hard part came at lunch when people started talking English."

Schmetz explained that the aspect of advertising he liked best was being with clients. "I think I was very good at working with our clients. I would make statements about 'value propositions' and 'engagement' and 'use cases' and they would nod their heads and then we'd go have a drink. Sometimes we'd go to Las Vegas and pretend to have a conference about social media, which I was really good at."

Asked why he decided to come forward with his admission at this time, Schmetz said, "It's time for me to move on. I feel like I've accomplished everything I can do here. But I want to apologize to my colleagues and clients. It was wrong of me to claim I understood anything. I have no idea why people buy stuff. I don't know what makes a good ad. I don't know anything. Honestly, I don't even know what an 'ecosystem' is. Is it like when you hear your own voice or something?"

When told of Schmetz's departure, one of his clients, Rajai Pargamanianaianan, CMO of Doodeo, said, "We are very sorry to see Fenton leave. He played an important role in our success. He had one of the most fertile marketing minds we've ever worked with. He deeply understood our value proposition and our engagement strategy and our use cases."

What is Schmetz going to miss most about advertising? "Oh, definitely the intellectual stimulation of trying to rearrange sentences to say the same thing everyone else is saying but in a much more complicated way. It's not as easy as you think. Also, I will miss the friendly girls."

What does he plan to do next? "I'm thinking of starting a blog."

STIMULATION NATION

We are addicted to stimulation.

Every bar has nine flat screens going at all times. Every commuter is wrapped in an iPhone-induced cocoon of digital entertainment, chat, or games. Every couch potato is checking his Facebook page while watching football. Every retail store has music playing and screens fluttering. Every sporting event is a non-stop parade of videos, promotions, and giveaways. Every movie is a hysterical spectacle of explosions, fire-breathing monsters, gunplay, and sex.

The stimulation is unrelenting.

We are so immersed in stimulation that when it ends we feel uncomfortable. It is no longer possible to vacation in quiet. Every resort swimming pool has pop music pumped in. Every hotel room has a huge television.

A great deal of this stimulation is supported and amplified by advertising. Everywhere we turn, there is advertising. You can't swing a dead social media consultant without hitting some. In addition to flooding all our traditional channels of communication, advertising has now saturated all our new media.

Against this background of constant stimulation and advertising overload we have the persistent chirping of new age marketing wizards and web hustlers.

First they told us that advertising was dead. When that observation proved to be astonishingly stupid they came up with another dubious premise. It goes something like this...

> *"The demise of in-your-face marketing and advertising is close at hand, to be replaced by...a form of advertising that depends on 'many lightweight interactions over time.' "*

This nonsense comes from a big shot at Facebook.

It is a tidy bit of verbal sleight-of-hand that accomplishes two objectives at once. First, it subtly acknowledges the dirty little secret that anyone with eyes can see, but no one wants to say out loud — that social media marketing has thus far been a weak advertising medium. But it cleverly tries to make the preposterous case that this weakness is actually a strength — that content marketing and social media are more effective because of their low impact.

There's only one problem with this lovely little fantasy — it is entirely without basis in fact. Where are the dominant brands that have been built with "many lightweight interactions over time?"

Where's the beer, or the airline, or the fast food joint, or the pick-up truck, or the cell phone, or the hotel chain, or the yogurt, or the sneakers, or the soda, or the car insurance, or the bank, or the...am I boring you?... that have been built with "lightweight interactions?"

I, too, would love to believe that there is a quieter, less frantic, more serene world in which subtlety and delicacy will carry the day. But where is the evidence?

The evidence is all in the other direction. We are a culture that is hooked on stimulation. We like our stimulation loud and we like it in hi def.

WHO THE HELL IS "THE CONSUMER?"

One of the things that gives me big chuckles is listening to marketing strategists talk about "the consumer."

"The consumer" is someone they think they know a lot about. Apparently she attends the same pilates classes as brand managers and goes on mountain bike rides with creative directors.

Despite their unctuous devotion to mouthing the word, most people in marketing don't know the first thing about "the consumer." This point was reinforced to me recently by two things I read. First was a blog piece by the great Dave Trott, writing about the reaction he gets to his cockney accent when speaking to business groups.

> *"Was the white collar world of marketing and senior management made up exclusively of middle class people with middle class accents? Did they think everyone, everywhere was exactly like them? Because here's a funny thing. Where I grew up everyone had cockney accents. Around three million people. And I'd lived my whole life without anyone ever commenting on it, until I started doing talks to people in marketing. People who, apparently, never hear anything but middle class accents."*

The second occurred when I was doing some research on automotive trends. I was reading a piece about how some cars stay in the hands of owners far longer than others. The writer of the piece thought he had uncovered a startling anomaly. He found that people with crappy cars held on to their cars longer than people with quality cars. Why would people hold on to lousy cars, he wanted to know?

He was digging around for explanations for this crazy fact. I'm pretty sure this would have stumped most marketing people.

So here's the answer Mr. Strategist — they hold on to their crappy cars longer because they don't have any fucking money.

Unlike us marketing wizards, people in the real world are forced to buy crappy things and hold onto them. To them, Walmart is a way of life. To us it's a punch line.

Here's something I wrote years ago in a piece called *Reality At The DMV...*

> *I'm thinking of making a monthly visit to the DMV a condition of employment for everyone on my staff. I want them to see what the people they're making ads for really look like. I want them to see the people they never see at the restaurants they go to; never see at the bars they frequent; never see at the focus groups they attend; and never hear from on Twitter. In other words, I want them to see the "consumer" they're all so very certain they know everything about.*

FACT FREE RESEARCH

I have often written about the lack of understanding of mathematics that plagues our industry. This is also true of our deficiencies in understanding research.

In the hard sciences, research is reasonably reliable because it measures things. In the soft (social) sciences, research is often not about measuring things, but about asking questions.

In other words, rather than watching to see if you're cheating on your wife, they ask you if you are. Then they treat your answer as a fact rather than just the bullshit it is.

The consequence of this is that a great many of the surveys, reports, and studies we read tell us nothing about what we're trying to understand, they tell us what people *say* about what we're trying to understand. A very different thing.

Here's an example:

A recent article in Ad Age on loyalty programs, reported that...

> *...The number spikes to 37% when it comes to millennials surveyed for the study, who said they would not be loyal to a brand that doesn't have a strong loyalty program...According to the study, 68% change when and where they make purchases to get loyalty rewards, and 60% will switch brands if incentivized.*

They use numbers and percents to pretend they have facts. There isn't a fact in sight. All they have is what people *say* they do. There is no more unreliable way to ascertain what people actually do than to ask them.

Like this...

A couple of years, ago Forbes ran an article with this headline: *CES: Survey Finds Traditional TV Viewing Is Collapsing.*

The "research" was done by Accenture, the consulting company. Listen to this frenzied nonsense from the report:

> *"...the number of consumers who watch broadcast or cable television in a typical week plunged to 48% in 2011 from 71% in 2009. Those are absolutely stunning results, which is (sic) accurate suggest that consumer behavior on television watching is changing faster than anyone had expected...Accenture's explanation for the trend is that the TV is losing ground to other devices – mobile phones, laptops and tablets..."*

All this hysteria was based on asking people questions, not measuring their behavior.

Fortunately, someone was actually measuring this behavior during this same period, so we can see how wrong the self-reported baloney was.

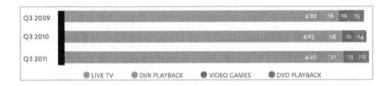

According to Nielsen's Cross-Platform report (Q3, 2013) TV viewing during the period of Accenture's "collapse" didn't change at all. The only thing that changed were the answers that people gave to Accenture's annoying survey takers.

Accenture's *"absolutely stunning results"* were stunning all right. Stunningly wrong.

THE SECOND SCREEN MYSTERY

Maybe you can help me understand something.

I often read that TV advertising isn't as powerful as it once was because people are sometimes distracted by other media while they're watching TV. They're tweeting, or they're on Facebook, or they are doing something else on line.

While I haven't seen any research that confirms this hypothesis, it seems logical to me and I think it's probably true.

Here's what I don't understand. Why isn't the same thing true for online advertising?

If a "second screen" distracts us from TV advertising, why doesn't it distract us from online advertising? If we're watching TV and we're on Facebook simultaneously, doesn't it seem curious that Facebook distracts us from TV ads but TV doesn't distract us from Facebook ads?

Is there something unique about online advertising that makes it immune to the second screen effect? If so, I'd love to know what that magical thing is.

If multi-tasking is really as damaging as our chattering media experts seem to think it is, then it is having a far more deleterious effect on online advertising than on TV.

Here's why.

We know how much time the average person spends watching TV and we know how much she spends on line. According to Nielsen's Cross-Platform Report for the 1st quarter of this year, the average adult (18+) spent about 36 hours a week watching TV and about 5 hours a week on line. I don't know how much time the average person spends doing both simultaneously, but it doesn't matter. Whatever the number is, it affects online advertising 7 times as much as it does TV advertising.

Let's say the average person spends 2 hours a week double-screening. That means she is distracted from TV by a second screen 2 hours out of 36, or about 6% of the time. But she is distracted from the web by a second screen 2 hours out of 5, or 40% of the time.

If you're bad at math, here's what it looks like visually.

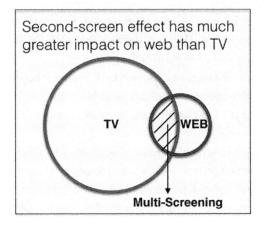

It's funny that I never hear about this from agency media experts or read about it in the trade press.

It couldn't be that these meatballs will thoughtlessly swallow and regurgitate any bullshit the online ad industry feeds them, could it?

Nah, I didn't think so.

THE DAY I WROTE A DIRTY BOOK

I spent my twenty-fifth birthday writing naughty literature.

At the time I was essentially a bum. I had quit my teaching job (by unanimous consent I was chosen The Worst Teacher In America) and had decided that I wanted to be a writer. Sadly, I had no idea what I wanted to write.

Scouring the classifieds, I answered an ad for a writer of "adult fiction." I submitted a sample and was hired.

You can imagine how proud I was.

Our office was in Greenwich Village. It was above a gym on 6th or 7th Av. somewhere south of West 4th St (decades of intervening cocktail parties, advertising meetings, and simulated adulthood have rendered the details a little hazy.)

There were three of us writing for this enterprise. First was a statuesque lesbian about a head taller than me who wore cat's eye glasses and was the sexiest thing I had ever laid eyes on. I still have dreams about the black knit dress she wore.

Then there was Erwin or Walter or something like that. He was a scrawny little intellectual about my age with curly, balding hair who walked bent over as if he was expecting the ceiling to fall in on him any moment.

And there was me. Since it was the 70's I had the obligatory full beard and shoulder length hair.

Our boss was a guy we will call James. He had an earring, which was unusual in those days. He was dressed like a character from the 70's in a bad TV show. He wore a multi-colored, vertically striped silk shirt with a long, pointy collar and rolled up sleeves. I wasn't sure if he owned the publishing company or was just the editor.

Our assignment was simple. We had to write a book a week. The book had to be exactly 150 pages, which meant we needed to write thirty pages a day. I can't *type* thirty pages a day. We got paid $1 a page.

I lasted one day.

When I tell this story, I often say that spending eight hours that day thinking about nothing but sex was too much, even for a mind like mine. But the truth is, one day's work exhausted everything I new about the subject.

I called in the second day and left a message that I wouldn't be returning. James called me back and asked me to reconsider. He said he had read my "manuscript" overnight and was very impressed.

Once again, you can imagine how proud I was.

I don't often talk about this episode. But sometimes, when people ask me what I did before advertising, I say, "I was a novelist."

WHY I TALK DIRTY

One of the questions I get about my blog is why I use naughty words so often when there are plenty of perfectly good polite ones that will do the job.

The question used to come from embarrassed (and worried) colleagues. And it still comes from my wife.

People tell me that dropping f-bombs and other 4-letter words on the blog costs me readers and credibility. That may be true. But I do it anyway.

Here's why. First, dirty words are not a big deal to me. Having grown up in New York City, every sentence was typically punctuated by an f-bomb. It's how I learned to think and how I talk and I don't see why I should change it when I write. It may not be pretty, but it's the real me.

Second, I think it's a healthy contrast to all the mealy-mouth bullshit being perpetrated by the newly corporatized, sanitized advertising industry. I don't mind being wrong but I do mind being timid. Naughty words have a use — they remove any hint of ambiguity.

Third, I think Americans are a little more prissy about language than is absolutely necessary. So, you see, I'm doing a public service.

Fourth, one of the great things about being an old fart is that I don't really give a shit what people think. If people don't like my language, I'm not going to worry about it. It's not that I'm trying to intentionally antagonize or irritate anyone, but I'm also not going to pretend I'm something I'm not to please anyone. It's one of the very few upsides of senile dementia.

MATH AND MILLENNIALS

Us ad hacks have a problem. We don't understand math.

The result is that we're easily impressed, mislead, and bullied by sneaky or irrelevant data, meaningless charts, fast talking metrics monkeys, and cement-head marketing mavens who know even less than we do.

Here's an example. Someone recently sent me one of those articles about the brilliance of auto makers shifting to online media to attract the precious Millennials. The piece featured this fact...

"Millennials, defined as 18 to 30 year olds, make up 40 percent of the total available car buying population..."

Wow! We better get our millennial strategy going pronto, right? Not so fast, amigo.

While they may make up 40% of the total *available* (that's the sneaky weasel word) car buying population, they make up a tiny percent of the *actual* car buying population.

In fact, the last stats I saw were that 18-34 year olds buy about 12% of new cars. So 18-30 year olds are probably about 10% of actual car buyers.

Let's go to the blackboard.

If 18-30 year olds are 40% of the *available* population but only 10% of *actual* buyers, that means they index at 25. That is, they buy 25% of what they would be expected to buy if they bought proportionately to their population.

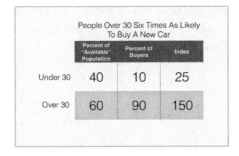

| | People Over 30 Six Times As Likely To Buy A New Car | | |
	Percent of "Available" Population	Percent of Buyers	Index
Under 30	40	10	25
Over 30	60	90	150

Meanwhile, people over 30 represent 60% of the available buyers and buy 90% of the cars. They index at 150. That means they buy 1.5 times as many cars as they should in a normal distribution.

So if this guy's numbers are correct, a person over 30 is *six times as likely* to buy a new car as someone under 30.

Still excited about that Millennial strategy, amigo?

THE CONSUMER IS IN CHARGE. OF WHAT?

"The Consumer Is In Charge" says Kaiser Permanente CIO.

"Consumers and their demands are in charge of business" says Frito-Lay's senior vice president and chief marketing officer.

"Today, the customer is in charge," said SrVP for marketing at Walmart.

One of the inescapable clichés of modern marketing is that "the consumer is in charge."

It's virtually impossible to talk with anyone in the marketing industry for any period of time without hearing this trite lump of nothing.

There are three things horribly wrong with it:

1. It assumes that there was a time in the past when the consumer *was not* in charge of making buying decisions. I'd love to know when that was.

2. It assumes the usual bullshit about the web having "changed everything."

3. Most depressingly, it shows a remarkable and frightening lack of understanding about what's really going on in the world.

Today, we are going to focus on item #3.

Among the most disturbing aspects of economics and society today is the alarming degree to which a handful of companies control what we see, hear, eat, and buy. Never before in my lifetime has so much power been consolidated into the hands of so few entities. Never before have the choices for consumers been so concentrated.

Here's a look at the food industry in the U.S.

According to the Huffington Post "These 10 Companies Control Enormous Number Of Consumer Brands"

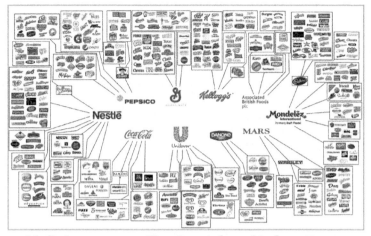

Media is even worse. Here is an infographic from 2012 reproduced by Business Insider, that claimed that 6 companies control 90% of the media in the U.S.

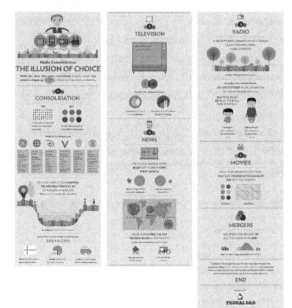

The financial industry is equally concentrated. Here's a chart from Mother Jones that shows how 37 banks became 4.

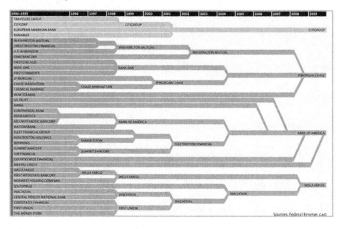

As for the mythical democratizing effect of the web, Google, Facebook and Yahoo dominate web traffic pretty effectively. Google alone is responsible for about 1/4 of all web traffic. And more than 50% of all web video is shared by YouTube and Netflix.

You have to do some truly monumental logic torturing to come up with a story in which all this consolidation and concentration of economic, marketing, and communication power leaves the consumer in charge.

More than ever in my lifetime, the big guys are driving the bus. The baloney about the consumer being in charge is just utopian digital rubbish.

SO YOU WANNA RUN AN AD AGENCY

If you're the typical wildly demented ad professional, you probably think that some day you'd like to run your own agency. Since I did that for several centuries I thought I'd give you a few tips

Managing an ad agency is like delivering a baby. It seems pleasant enough in theory. But until you've actually done it you have no idea how messy it is.

Forget everything you've ever seen on Mad Men. Running an ad agency will not make you intriguing, handsome, or sexy. I suggest you Google a photo of me.

There are only two types of people who work at ad agencies — crazy people and people training to be crazy.

From where you sit now, your colleagues seem good-natured and sensible. When you're their employer, you will soon find that all the good-natured and sensible people are working over at Subway making pastrami melts.

One day someone you have worked with happily for 10 years will come into your office and close the door. She will tell you that she has left her husband and two children. She has fallen in love with your biggest client and is now living in the back of his 4-Runner. As soon as he tells his wife about this (which will happen "any day now") they will be moving to Oregon to make leather candles.

One afternoon you will be on a conference call among several of your staff and a film production company. The production company's director will be going on and on about how much he loves the storyboard they're bidding on. While he's doing this, your agency producer will be entertaining the troops by using his right hand to make the universal gesture for "whack-off." Two weeks later a letter will arrive by messenger informing you that a legal action has been instituted against you for enabling a hostile work environment.

One morning at 3:30 am your home phone will ring. It will be the nice young Stanford graduate you hired in your billing department.

He has been arrested for shooting off a gun at a strip club. It's all a terrible mistake, but can you come downtown and bail him out?

You will think of your agency as "your team." And, like all teams, they will have a limitless capacity for petty grievances and will go out of their way to undermine each other.

Running an ad agency has nothing to do with making ads, working with clients, or managing accounts.

Your only real job is to keep crazy people from killing each other.

.

ADVERTISING NEEDS TROUBLEMAKERS

The advertising industry has become too respectable, too congenial, and too polite.

We are in desperate need of troublemakers. We need shit disturbers. We need hell-raisers.

We need the kind of quarrelsome, pugnacious, opinionated people that make the arts vibrant and interesting.

There's way too much consensus. Way too much cordiality. Way too little controversy.

Attending an advertising conference these days is like going to an insurance seminar. It is full of bland, head-nodding jargon-monkeys who are very keen on tweeting out the conventional blather of smug "experts."

Nobody seems inclined to challenge the wearisome assertions of modern-day wizards, no matter how many times they've been wrong.

It's all backwards. Rebelliousness is supposed to be a characteristic of youth. But the only people I hear wailing about the insufferable tedium of ad-think these days are old fools like me.

It ain't supposed to be this way. We need people who aren't afraid to get up on stage at the next "big data" conference and pull their pants down.

We need people who aren't afraid to break a layout over a client's head.

We need people who give a shit.

You know what you call people who give a shit? Troublemakers.

About The Author

Bob Hoffman is an author, speaker, and partner in Type A Group, LLC, a company that consults to marketers, advertisers and media.

 He is author of *101 Contrarian Ideas About Advertising*, *The Ad Contrarian* and *The Ad Contrarian* blog, which was named one of the world's most influential advertising and marketing blogs by Business Insider.

Bob founded and was chairman/ceo of Hoffman/Lewis advertising. He retired from Hoffman/Lewis in 2013.

In 2012, Bob was selected "Ad Person of the Year" by the San Francisco Advertising Club.

Previously, Bob was ceo of Mojo USA and president and creative director of Allen & Dorward.

Bob has created advertising for McDonald's, Toyota, Shell, Nestle, Blue Cross, Chevrolet, Pepsico, Bank of America, AT&T, and more companies than he cares to think about.

He has served on several boards including the Advertising and Marketing International Network, and spent a year as Special Assistant to the Executive Director of the California Academy of Sciences.

Bob is a frequent speaker at industry conferences, business meetings, advertising events, and long liquid lunches.